HOW TO SURVIVE IN AN UPSIDE DOWN ECONOMY

GEORGE NEWMAN

Blossom Valley Press
P.O. Box 32133
Tucson, AZ 85751-2133
Phone: 520-325-1224
email: argonnel@gmail.com

Typesetting and cover design: Susan Leonard, Rose Island Bookworks

ISBN 978-0-939894-03-1

Library of Congress Control Number: 2016933276

Manufactured, typeset and printed in the United States of America

In Memory of Mike Kelly

Acknowledgements

For superb editing, my thanks go to Marian Sanders and Mack Lundstrom.

I'm indebted to Susan Leonard of Rose Island Bookworks for outstanding cover and interior design and to Jim Brown of jimandzetta.com for expertly guiding me through the challenges of Print on Demand (POD) and e-book publishing.

Also to publishing attorney Brad Bunin and Charles Luebbering, CPA, for their sage counsel and advice.

To Carrie Spencer for her attractive and efficient design of the website and Barbara Brabec for generously sharing her publishing experiences.

I'm grateful to Margaret York, Dale Rodebaugh, Meg O'Connor and Rick Newman for painstaking proofreading.

Finally, my love and thanks to Sondra Newman, my wife and in-house editor, for her patience, optimism, support and encouragement during the writing of this book.

Warning — Disclaimer

The information contained in this book is designed to provide information on the subjects discussed. It is sold with the understanding that the publisher and author are not engaged in rendering legal, accounting or other professional services or advice. If legal or other expert assistance or advice is required, the services of a competent professional should be sought before making any decisions or taking any actions.

The content of each article or item is the sole expression and opinion of the author. There may exist many differing opinions, and it is the responsibility of the reader to determine which opinion, if any, suits his or her individual needs.

Self-employment is not a get-rich-quick scheme. Anyone who decides to elect this option must expect to invest a lot of time and effort into it. For many people, self-employment might not be the right choice. These individuals should discuss this issue with members of their family and their closest advisors before making a decision.

Every effort has been made to make this book as complete and as accurate as possible. However, there may be mistakes, both typographical and in content. Therefore, this text should be used only as a general guide and not as an ultimate source on this subject. Furthermore, this manual contains information that is current only up to the printing date.

The purpose of this manual is to inform. No warranties or guarantees are expressed or implied by the publisher's choice to include any of the content in this volume. Neither the publisher nor the author shall be liable for any physical, psychological, emotional, financial, or commercial damages, including, but not limited to, special, incidental, consequential or other damages. Our views and rights are the same: You are responsible for your own choices, actions, and results.

If you do not wish to be bound by the above, you may return this book to the publisher for a full refund.

Table of Contents

The Parable of the Coach
by Edward Bellamy

By way of attempting to give the reader some general impression of the way people lived together in those days, and especially of the relations of the rich and poor to one another, perhaps I cannot do better than to compare society as it then was to a prodigious coach which the masses of humanity were harnessed to and dragged toilsomely along a very hilly and sandy road.

The driver was hunger, and permitted no lagging, though the pace was necessarily very slow. Despite the difficulty of drawing the coach at all along so hard a road, the top was covered with passengers who never got down, even at the steepest ascents. These seats at the top were very breezy and comfortable. Well up out of the dust, their occupants could enjoy the scenery at their leisure, or critically discuss the merits of the straining team.

Naturally such places were in great demand and the competition for them was keen, every one seeking as the first end of life to secure a seat on the coach for himself and to leave it to his child after him. By the rule of the coach a man could leave his seat to whom he wished, but on the other hand there were so many accidents by which it might at any time be wholly lost.

For all that they were so easy, the seats were very insecure, and at every sudden jolt of the coach persons were slipping out of them and falling to the ground, where they were instantly compelled to take hold of the rope and help to drag the coach on which they had before ridden so pleasantly. It was naturally regarded as a terrible misfortune to lose one's seat, and the apprehension that this might happen to them or their friends was a constant cloud upon the happiness of those who rode.

But did they think only of themselves? you ask. Was not their very luxury rendered intolerable to them by comparison with the lot of their brothers and sisters in the harness, and the knowledge that their own weight added to the toil? Had they no compassion for fellow beings from whom fortune only distinguished them?

Oh, yes, commiseration was frequently expressed by those who rode for those who had to pull the coach, especially when the vehicle came to a bad place on the road, as it was constantly doing, or to a particularly steep hill. At such times, the desperate straining of the team, their agonized leaping and plunging under the pitiless lashes of hunger, the many who fainted at the rope and were trampled in the mire, made a very distressing spectacle, which often called forth highly creditable displays of feeling on the top of the coach. At such times the passengers would call down encouragingly to the toilers of the rope, exhorting them to patience, and holding out hopes of possible compensation in another world for the hardness of their lot, while others contributed to buy salves and liniments for the crippled and injured.

It was agreed that it was a great pity that the coach should be so hard to pull, and there was a sense of general relief when the specially bad piece of road was gotten over. The relief was not, indeed, wholly on account of the team, for there was always some danger at these bad places of a general overturn in which all would lose their seats.

It must in truth be admitted that the main effect of the spectacle of the misery of the toilers at the rope was to enhance the passengers' sense of value of their seats upon the coach, and to cause them to hold on to them more desperately than before. If the passengers could only have felt assured that neither they nor their friends would ever fall from the top, it is probable that, beyond contributing to the funds for liniments and bandages, they would have troubled themselves extremely little about those who dragged the coach.

Introduction

A couple years ago, when my wife and I were returning home to Tucson from a trip to California, we stopped overnight in Chandler, a growing suburb along the southeastern edge of Phoenix. We were hungry.

A desk clerk at the motel recommended a nearby Italian restaurant located in a sprawling upscale shopping center.

Outside the restaurant were dozens of parked, late-model vehicles, mostly SUVs. It was a weekend, and inside I saw that all the tables were filled with what appeared to be upwardly mobile individuals, most in their twenties, thirties and early forties. Many were seated as a family, and the tables were laden with appetizing food and drink. Everyone seemed to be enjoying the moment. Judging from the scene, one might believe he had entered Prosperityville.

What struck me as strange, however, was that I knew that at that same moment there were perhaps thousands of individuals living within a few miles who stayed at home that evening because they were unemployed and had no money to go out anywhere. This experience occurred at the peak of the subprime mortgage debacle and subsequent economic recession. The Phoenix area was among the nation's hardest hit.

The contrast I witnessed brought back memories of Edward Bellamy's *The Parable of the Coach*.

As you read this, you might wonder why a how-to book would begin with a parable from a utopian novel published more than a century ago. To answer that, let me start by asking if you've read *The Parable of the Coach* or simply skipped over it? If you read it, what impact did it have? If you haven't read it, I urge you to go back and do so right now or you'll be missing a critical factor needed for your survival plan.

Okay, now that we're all on board, can you fathom that you've possibly lost your seat on the coach? And that what pertained in 1887 when Bellamy published his futuristic novel still holds true today?

Perhaps, before you were laid off from that good-paying job, you never envisioned yourself as holding a seat on Bellamy's metaphoric coach. But, now that it's becoming apparent that you are on the ground toiling at the rope while some of your friends and co-workers remain atop the coach, you are likely feeling a bit of resentment. You might have to turn down invitations to join your friends for weekends in Las Vegas or explain to the kids why there's no money to send them to computer camp this summer. Or give up the weekly golf game. It's painful, and in some cases depressing. And it seems so unfair. What have you done to deserve it?

Chances are that you served your company well, earned good reviews and would still be working today were it not for the fact that your job was shipped overseas or your company was acquired by a bigger fish which consolidated jobs resulting in thousands of layoffs, etc. Or perhaps it was that your hair is turning gray.

But here you are, displaced in your forties or fifties, accustomed to living at a comfortable standard that your previous salary could easily support, and now you're looking at a stack of unpaid bills in one pile and rejection letters from prospective employers in another.

Indeed this condition can be described as no less than traumatic for the individual who is experiencing it

In August 2013, *Money* magazine reported that one in seven Americans was either out of a job or working fewer hours than they wanted.

At about the same time, a data analysis coordinated by Washington University in St. Louis found four out of five U.S.

adults struggling with joblessness, near poverty or reliance on welfare.

Also at around the same time, it was reported that 47 million Americans are receiving food stamps, a new record.

The Associated Press, which cited the data, concluded that the figures point "to an increasingly globalized U.S. economy, the widening gap between rich and poor and loss of good-paying manufacturing jobs" as reasons for the trend.

In 2014, Rutgers University released results of a national study titled "Unhappy, Worried and Pessimistic: Americans in the Aftermath of the Great Recession."

These are some conclusions of the study:

- Despite sustained job growth and lower levels of unemployment, most Americans don't think the economy has improved in the last year or that it will in the next.
- Just one in six Americans believes that job opportunities for the next generation will be better than for their generation; five years ago, four in ten held that view.
- Roughly four in five Americans have little or no confidence that the federal government will make progress on the nation's most important problems over the next year.
- 16 percent of the public, or 38 million people, were "devastated" because they experienced a "major, permanent" change in the quality of their life.
- 19 percent, or 46 million, were "downsized" due to "permanent but minor" changes in standards of living.
- 10 percent, or 24 million, were "set back," experiencing "major, but temporary" changes in their quality of life.

- 22 percent, or 53 million, were "troubled" by the recession and endured only a "minor and temporary" change
- Only one in three of the nation's 240 million adults reported that they were completely "unscathed" by the recession.

In February 2016, *The Los Angeles Times* reported that nearly one-third of U.S. heads of households ages 55 and older have no pension or retirement savings and that eight in ten Americans say they will work well into their 60s or skip retirement entirely.

Are there underlying causes for this overwhelming pessimism?

There are many causes such as dependence on imported energy, continued loss of good-paying jobs to offshore locations and failure to protect jobs here, failure to deal with illegal immigration, increasing indebtedness by both government and ordinary citizens, imbalance of trade and failure to distinguish between renewable and non-renewable resources, to name a few. Of course, the list is much longer.

From these and other irrefutable data, I've concluded that we are living in an *upside down economy.* Others have termed it "The New Normal." And no one whose opinion I've read in the press or spoken with personally expects things to improve much anytime soon.

What about the promise of "retraining" that we read about so often? In August of 2014, in a front-page story, *The New York Times* reported that many of these graduates, after taking courses lasting as long as two years, are worse off than when they started, "mired in unemployment and debt from training for positions that do not exist and working elsewhere for minimum wage."

If you haven't seen these two movies — *Up in the Air* starring George Clooney and *Company Men* with Tommy Lee Jones in the lead role — you should view both at home. They're available through Netflix or overnight rental. Both paint a realistic picture of what one can expect when they are in middle age and have lost good-paying jobs.

I could share some additional thoughts with you about why I'm convinced that as a nation we are where we are today — on a downward economic spiral despite the current hoopla about new jobs being added. But I have decided it's far more important to get right down to the business of providing you with the strategies you need to lift yourself out of this abyss and come out wiser and stronger than before.

This book is divided into three main parts:

- *Toward Independence and Security*
- *How to Start Your Own Business*
- *How to Save Money*

Not only will the strategies I'll share with you on the following pages help you to survive and restore your life to a level of normalcy and security, but you will begin to derive an inner satisfaction each time you successfully employ one of these tips and discover that it has worked for you.

Every time you chalk up a success, you'll say to yourself, "I don't need corporate employment. No one can hold life or death power over my future. No one can fire me. No one can hand me a layoff notice. I'm my own boss and I can do it!"

You're trading pressure, stress and heavy-duty uncertainty for economic stability and peace of mind.

This then begs the question: Is it worth it to you to rid yourself of this bogus notion that an individual must do everything that he can to maintain a certain high economic and social standing — regardless of the cost to your nervous system — in exchange for a less stressful life where you are the master of your time?

Many will answer "yes." But, I must caution you. This is not for everyone.

The strategies in this book will work only if you're a self-starter. You must maintain dedication, perseverance and persistence to succeed as an independent business owner. You'll need self-discipline and willingness to work long hours. You'll need to make sacrifices.

Understandably, not everyone is adaptable to taking on the responsibility for starting one's own business. For those who would find this option unsuitable or in some situations impossible, I refer you to The Door County Model described in Chapter 44 of this book, which offers an alternative approach. It's more about jobs — mostly part-time jobs — rather than independent business.

But, before you rule out the possibility of self-employment, consider this:

Do you know anyone nowadays who is working 9 to 5? Five days a week? You're most likely to find this if that person is employed by a government agency. For almost everyone else, set or fixed hours are only a memory. In the private sector most employees are now expected to work as many hours as it requires to get the job done. But the pay remains the same. No overtime. And often you're expected to come in for a half a day on Saturdays, also uncompensated.

If you're working for a corporation, the new normal also includes workers routinely being laid off. Those who remain are expected to do their work as well as the work of their co-workers who were laid off. Thus longer hours.

As a result, the corporation declares increased profits and the CEO who has put this plan into motion receives a million-dollar bonus for cutting payroll expense.

And what do you receive? You're told that you're lucky to have a job, and if you're not satisfied, the company can find someone else to do your work.

Money magazine, citing a recent Gallup poll, reported that the average full-time salaried employee puts in nearly 10 hours daily. Worse yet, 25 percent of those polled say they regularly work a 60-hour week.

In February, 2015, *The New York Times* reported that about 1.7 million people, on average, lose their jobs every month.

Given these circumstances and considering the difficulty of again securing employment if you are laid off, why not consider working those long hours on your own behalf and get paid for it?

As a personal disclosure, I'd like to inform you that this is not simply a timely topic that I've chosen to write about. I've lived this way most of my adult life and continue to do so.

It was many years ago that I found myself in your shoes, and my sole regret is that I didn't make my move to independence even sooner.

My role model at the time was an old friend who often declared that he could survive a huge financial fall and quickly come back to recover. He challenged anyone to take him up on his offer of a bet. I remember him saying, "You can blindfold me and drop me off in any town or city in America. All I ask is that you let me keep a $50 bill in my pocket so I can get a room somewhere that night and won't be arrested for loitering. By the next morning, I'll be earning money and getting back on my feet. All I need is my health." Needless to say, his degree of confidence left an impression.

Before I get into the specific strategies for recovery, I must emphasize that every money-making tip won't bear fruit. That's why I favor businesses that require no startup capital. You might need to launch three or four ventures over the course of a year and test which one(s) serve you best. It's not uncommon for independent business people to carry business cards in their pocket for each of their various small businesses.

A recent study by the Kauffman Foundation, whose goal is the advancement of entrepreneurship, reported that persons aged 45 and older started 48 percent of new businesses, but accounted for 64 percent of firms surviving four years.

If you're reading this book and are currently employed full time, I refer you to Chapter 77 which can serve as one of your "insurance policies" if in the future you receive a layoff notice. Part-time entrepreneurs can benefit from all of the tips in the *How to Start Your Own Business* part of this book as well as the many *How to Save Money* strategies.

Finally, one of the most valuable pieces of advice I ever received was given to me by a mentor many years ago. He said often that one of the keys to success in life is knowing when to hang in and when to let go.

Let's get started.

Tucson, Arizona
January 2016

Part I

Toward Independence and Security

1.

Survival and Self-Esteem

If you're currently unemployed or underemployed and are struggling to pay your bills, then you're undoubtedly aware that you're facing not one but *two* major challenges.

The first — financial distress — is of course the most obvious.

The second — a blow to your self-esteem — can cause injury just as severe as the first. Sometimes, even more. But, it's one of those issues that folks seldom talk about.

Make no mistake: unemployment is not just about money. When you lose your job and are out of work, there's almost always going to be a financial pinch. But, it's the self-esteem part that makes things even more traumatic.

When we talk about self-esteem in this context, what we're saying is that often *your job defines who you are.*

Right now, you might be thinking, "Before I was laid off, I was a somebody. Now, I'm a nobody."

This might not hold true if you've been working in a low-level job under conditions that were less than desirable. But, what if you've worked in a position for a number of years and held responsibility? Your fall will be an even harder fall because it's a descent from a higher position, such as a seat on the metaphoric coach that you read about at the start of this book.

Unless you're very lucky, it's unlikely that you'll get your former position back or one that pays anything like the one you previously held.

You can continue searching for that coveted job that no longer exists, often sending out resumes for many months without a single positive reply or opt for the alternative path, which if successful, can bring with it even greater satisfaction and a heightened sense of self-esteem. That path is being on your own, and it leads you to being a successful independent businessman or businesswoman.

Yes, you *can* go back to being a somebody. And you'll be a somebody because you'll be the owner and CEO of an independent business that no one can take away from you just by moving a pin on a map posted at corporate headquarters.

In the ensuing pages, I'll lead you step-by-step through what you need to know to make that goal a reality. I wish to remind you that I've been there myself.

> **Never, never, never give up.**
>
> ***– Winston Churchill***

2.

Attitude is Everything

To achieve economic stability as well as the restoration of your self-esteem, you'll need a complete makeover and a new attitude to complement it.

I once met a man who had pulled himself up from the depths after being dumped from a responsible position. He had worked for the company for 28 years and saw his job exported to China. He told me that while on his road to recovery he saw himself as the quarterback of a football team and that his mission was to inspire his teammates (his family) in a sustained drive toward his opponent's goal line. "You must remain relentless and of single purpose of mind," he declared.

This approach requires constant and full attention to the goal with no slacking off, no timeouts. Admittedly, not everyone can do it. But, for those who are already self-starters by nature and others who can learn to be, the payoff is rewarding and the feeling that comes with it is liberating. Say goodbye to bosses who tell you when you can do this or when you can go there. Now, all the responsibility is on your shoulders. You will become the boss of... you.

Every morning you must psych yourself to face the challenges of the day. At the end of most days though, you'll feel a huge amount of inner satisfaction, much more than you ever did when you worked for someone else.

3.

Everyone Needs In

If you have a spouse or a family, it's likely that by this time you have informed them of the economic changes affecting the household. In a few cases that information might be sufficient to rally the troops and ensure that everyone is on board and prepared to work hard and make sacrifices. But, in the majority of households, it doesn't seem to work out that way.

Your greatest challenge will be enabling the kids to understand. If there are two parents in the household, they need to work in tandem to help the children grasp the situation. Children are by nature egocentric and need to be approached from several different directions. You'll find that those children who have been given responsibility at an early age, such as helping with household chores, generally respond more positively than those who haven't.

Sometimes, creative approaches can be introduced to help children understand the situation. Often, especially with younger children, this can be achieved through the use of metaphor or simile, such as reading aloud to them *The Parable of the Coach*, after which you explain that Mommy or Daddy has lost their seat on the coach through no fault of their own.

You can further explain that this can happen to any parent nowadays and that they need not feel ashamed because in these hard economic times the parents of many other children with whom they're acquainted can also lose their seats.

You'll find that the more you bring your kids in on the game plan the more likely they are to participate, often at a level you might not expect.

Certainly, there will be children, often teenagers, who will resist joining the team, citing their need for their smartphones, texting and activity on social media. An appropriate answer for those teens is "Okay, if you don't want to help support the family, we'll manage without you. But if you want to continue keeping up with what you believe you have to do to blend in with your classmates, then you'll need to find part-time work to pay for it. Or maybe you'd like to help us plan our budget and tell us how much should be set aside for food and how much for texting and cellphones."

Because teens and pre-teens tend to be the least understanding, you'll find that they'll require the most attention. Rarely will a spouse fail to accept that the family, *at least temporarily,* will have to live under reduced circumstances. You're most likely to see this happen when one of the partners has married for money — and when the money is no longer there, it's time to depart.

If you can cross this bridge with everyone working together, you're virtually assured of success. Admittedly, easier said than done.

4.

Who Are Your Real Friends?

When disaster strikes, you quickly find out who your real friends are. Often, the revelations might surprise you.

A laid-off accountant told me that she always thought that she could count on her "best friend," a woman her own age with whom she shared both her interests and her confidences. It turned out that when the laid-off accountant confided to her "best friend" that she was in need, the friend responded with the often-used "If there's anything I can do..." and wasn't heard from again.

Meanwhile, a woman, who for years performed part-time domestic duties in the accountant's household, began bringing over casseroles, fresh fruit and home-baked cookies. She even offered to work for reduced pay through the crunch. The accountant declined, but felt fortunate to have discovered the depth of this woman's caring and character.

Unless you've found yourself in a similar pinch before, you won't know who are your real friends and which ones are merely acquaintances.

Don't waste a lot of time on the latter, but do acknowledge those who come to assist you and remember to be around for them in their time of need.

5.

Talk to People

While the concept of networking is likely not new to anyone reading this, the importance of networking groups, especially for the unemployed or underemployed, now takes on greater meaning.

When I gave up my weekly paycheck, I was recently divorced and was about as alone as anyone can be. Besides sheer determination, what helped pull me through was a monthly networking breakfast which I had been attending regularly.

In all, there were about two dozen men and women who formed the core of this particular group, and usually no more than 12 to 15 would be present at any one sitting.

The meetings were held at a coffee shop in a low-rent district of San Jose, California, and the owner always combined enough tables to seat everyone without splitting the group.

The sessions were lively and engaging. Participants were encouraged to think outside the box.

Almost everyone who attended was either self-employed or the sole owner of a small business. Today new vocabulary words such as "solopreneur" have been created to describe such independent workers and "microbusiness" for enterprises with one to four employees.

What immediately struck me as heartening was to see how members of the group offered to help others with problems, including problems that were not always related to business.

Often, I'd hear words such as these: "My brother-in-law knows the gatekeeper at that company (or state office or medical office, etc.). I'll ask him to get you an appointment to see the manager."

Time and time again I saw members resolve their problems through networking over coffee, toast and scrambled eggs.

Now, there are thousands of different support groups online, but I've found that there's still no substitute for face-to-face meetings.

Networking breakfasts usually meet early and don't take time away from the normal work day.

They are usually inexpensive, and if necessary you can get by with an order of toast and a cup of coffee.

I made some lifelong friends through those breakfasts, which I can't attend any more since my wife and I moved to Tucson.

If you don't know of such a group, start one yourself. Invite two friends initially — ones you enjoy being with and have life experiences to share. Next month, ask them to bring along anyone they think might benefit. People will come and go, but you'll have your core group, and it can change your life.

> **Do you want to know who you are?**
> **Don't ask. Act!**
> **Action will delineate and define you.**
>
> ***– Thomas Jefferson***

6.

Is Your House Underwater?

Determining whether to let your house be taken back by the lender could be one of the more important decisions you make.

This is of course assuming that you currently live in a mortgaged home and it is still underwater.

Because there are so many factors and contingencies that go into such a decision, it's all but impossible to provide specific advice here.

Perhaps, the best and least costly way to approach this is to contact a real estate agent you know, and if you don't know one personally, then ask your friends for a referral.

Most agents who have been in the business for a length of time are fully familiar with all the ins and outs related to the dilemma of "underwater" houses.

Much will depend on issues such as whether you are intending to file for bankruptcy, move to another locale and whether your monthly payments are far beyond an amount you can currently afford for housing. And there are, of course, other considerations.

Under certain circumstances, the agent might recommend asking the lender for approval of a short sale. However, if you decide to do this, be aware that whatever amount of mortgage forgiveness you receive from the lender might be considered *income* by the IRS, and you could be taxed on that amount. For a time, Congress provided a tax exemption under these circumstances, so be sure to discuss this aspect with your accountant or tax advisor. A mistake or failure to be informed of changes in the law could be costly.

Clouding all of the issues are current court cases and new legislation that impose a stricter burden on the lender or his agent to prove ownership before proceeding with foreclosure. As noted above, there is also legislation, both pending and approved, to ease the tax burden on those who have lost their homes and have received some form of mortgage forgiveness.

Many of you are already aware that this issue and its attendant consequences and fallout are all due to the subprime mortgage debacle in which mortgages were packaged into bundles, then sliced into small pieces and sold to unwitting investors and institutions.

One of the many consequences stemming from this phenomenon is that when homeowners who want to remain in their houses make an offer to restructure their loans, the agent or service company can't respond in a timely fashion, if at all, because it would require approval of sometimes as many as a dozen or more investors or institutions that bought a slice of a particular mortgage package.

Ironically, this has set up a situation where foreclosure of a house for non-payment has been stalled for sometimes years while awaiting resolution.

However, it also creates an opportunity for those living in the home to continue residing there without paying any more money to the lender. The dweller continues to pay monthly utilities and remains in the house until receiving a notice from the sheriff to vacate. Often that can take years and during that time the dweller can stockpile some cash for times ahead when a move is required.

When making your decision, first gather all the information you can get your hands on pertinent to your individual situation. Then carefully sift through it together with your spouse or a close friend or advisor. Finally, when you've reached a tentative decision, contact all those who provided you with advice and say, "I've come to a tentative decision. This is what I'm considering doing. Please tell me if this is not the best course to take and if so, tell me what I should be doing instead and why."

Then, when you've passed that point, run your decision by a qualified accountant and if possible, a lawyer who is an expert on this subject. You can't afford a mistake here.

> **If you don't design your own life plan, chances are you'll fall into someone else's plan. And guess what they have planned for you? Not much.**
>
> ***– Jim Rohn***

7.

Bankruptcy — Yes or No?

Many people who have suffered loss of a job will find themselves considering bankruptcy. Unless you are among those who are fortunate enough to have a sound financial foundation beneath you and are able to sustain yourself for an indefinite period, you may be among them.

Even if you decide not to file for bankruptcy, it might be in your interest to consult with a bankruptcy attorney. Here are some of those reasons.

First, assuming that you are not currently renting, your decision will depend on the status of your house or condo. Is it currently underwater? Has the interest rate reset to a much higher rate than when you purchased the property? Can you afford to continue making the payments? Although this subject has been covered in an earlier chapter, it is certain to come up when the issue of bankruptcy is discussed, and you should be prepared with facts and figures.

Next, you must keep in mind that whether you file for bankruptcy, have your mortgage foreclosed or agree to a short sale of your house, your credit rating is likely to be negatively affected.

You will notice throughout this book that I strongly recommend that you become debt free as quickly as possible and take on no further credit debt of any kind. Being debt free is critical to successfully implementing your survival plan.

The only exception to this debt-free strategy is that you maintain a credit card, preferably a VISA card, which you will need in your business and for personal matters, etc. Of course, your balance needs to be paid in full each month to avoid high interest rates and fees.

If you decide to file for bankruptcy, you should contact your credit card issuer and let them know that you are filing for bankruptcy but that you intend to continue paying your credit card bill on time each month. According to individuals I've talked with who have done this, in most cases, I'm told, the credit card issuers did not cancel their cards, especially when their accounts were in good standing.

However, when you file for bankruptcy you must list *all* of your debts. So, if you have a remaining balance on your credit card, you would need to list it, and it's likely that your credit card issuer would be notified, which might under certain circumstances prove to be a problem. Your credit card issuer might anticipate that you'll be discharging in bankruptcy this current debt along with all the others.

The solution to this potential problem is to be sure that you've fully paid off any balance on the card that you wish to keep and that you have made a monthly payment on time to take care of the current balance. This way, when you are filling out bankruptcy forms you won't need to list the credit card issuer in question because at that moment you'll have zero debt with that issuer.

And since you're required to list every debt, you must also include items like dry cleaning bills or car repairs. Although those debts will be among the entire list of dischargeable debts, there's no law that prevents you from later making arrangements to pay these individuals a small amount at a time. You should let them know in advance of your intentions because each will receive a notice of the bankruptcy filing. The arrangement enables you to protect independent merchants who could be hurt and may be among your neighbors and friends. You might not feel the same about debts to mortgage companies, large corporations and public utilities.

Living debt free and buying only what you can afford to pay for at time of purchase represents a marked divergence from a lifestyle to which most Americans are accustomed, and it might not be an easy task to make the switch. But, once you've accomplished it you'll sleep much better and never wish to go back to the old habit of saying, "Charge it."

If you file for bankruptcy, it's quite likely that you'll be unable to qualify for a mortgage for years to come and that many creditors will turn down your applications. Yes, there are drawbacks.

But, before you consult a bankruptcy attorney, I recommend that you discuss this issue with your inner circle, those folks whom you trust to make good decisions and perhaps also have some knowledge or experience in this realm.

After doing so, arrange a consultation with an attorney who specializes in bankruptcy, *not* with a general practice lawyer. There are bankruptcy specialists in almost every town and city in America, and most will provide an initial consultation without charge. However, be sure to ask in advance about this and if there is a charge, how much.

Bring all your relevant papers and documents and ask to discuss the pros and cons of filing for bankruptcy as they pertain to you.

Of course, you will also want to know if there is a package fee for the bankruptcy and the amount. For obvious reasons, most bankruptcy lawyers will require that the fee be paid upfront.

You may even be advised that you would be better off not filing for bankruptcy, and the attorney will tell you the reasons why.

However, it will serve you well to get a second opinion, not only for the purpose of benefiting from that second lawyer's experience, but you might also find a significant difference in the two lawyer's fees or in their years of experience.

And if life isn't complicated enough, you need to know that there exists another variety of lawyer specialists, the asset protection attorney.

If you're being hassled by creditors or possibly face being sued, or if you are considering bankruptcy — and there is some property you want to protect — you might need to consider making an appointment with an asset protection lawyer. An example of this could be that your wife and her sister co-own a duplex or small garden apartment and you want to protect it from creditors.

In such a case, you would want to consult with an asset protection attorney first, perhaps followed up by your consultation with the bankruptcy lawyer.

You will usually find asset protection lawyers in larger metropolitan areas whereas bankruptcy lawyers can be found in most American towns and cities.

Again a word of caution: Tread carefully in these areas as a single mistake can be very costly and can impact your life for many years to come.

And remember, there's no substitute for experience. Consult only with those experts who are recommended and have years of experience under their belts.

8.

Time Management

There is no single factor that is more critical to your recovery and future solvency than time management.

In short, how you manage your time will determine your success.

You've heard the saying that the three most important things to take into account when buying real estate are: location, location and location.

Well, when it comes to surviving in an upside down economy, it's time management, time management and time management.

Please take this advice to heart, because if you're prone to frittering away your time watching TV or videos, playing electronic games or texting your friends with minutiae or trivia, your chances of succeeding with an economic recovery program are somewhere between zero and nil.

To succeed, given these adverse conditions, requires an intense focus and commitment, unlike any to which you've been previously accustomed.

It means that you need to make every waking moment count.

It means invoking some very basic principles such as achieving efficiencies in shopping and grouping errands in clusters, reducing mileage and commutes, etc.

The time you save by implementing these efficiencies is time that you can use to grow your independent business.

Within those parameters, you need to establish a rank order of priorities. It might go something like this:

- Reserve your most productive working hours for responding to customer calls and servicing customers. Make every effort to accommodate customers in the shortest time possible. Consider this period "prime time."

- When you're not actually engaged in customer activity, be working on or thinking of ways to expand your business or businesses.

- When you're not on prime time, such as in the evenings, you might investigate some of the many money-saving opportunities. However, remember that while you can save a few dollars using money-savers, they do not compare in net productivity (i.e., dollars) to what you can earn through your business or some part-time or temporary employment. When one of these opportunities arises, be it day or night, drop the money-saver, put it on hold and switch over to the *money-earner.*

- Of course, you'll need to set aside time for relaxation or play, which can be accommodated when you see a lull in the action. When I was living in California and operating as a one-man band (figuratively speaking), I once worked for 14 days consecutively, before a fellow independent like myself and I decided to take a day off in the middle of the week and drive to a state redwood park for a day's hiking. That day was all we needed to get back to our fledgling businesses with renewed spirit.

Finally, keep in mind the saying "*Time is money.*" You need to remind yourself of those words every time you find yourself absorbed with some diversion that isn't geared to move your economic future forward.

9.

Keeping One Step Ahead

Another key to gaining economic independence is keeping well informed. My Great-Uncle Max instilled this in me when I was in my early twenties.

We lived many miles apart, but we spoke at length via phone at least once a month. Uncle Max always gave me good advice. He would end every phone conversation with these words: "My boy, remember, you must always keep one step ahead of the crowd. One step ahead. Don't forget this."

To do this, it isn't just a matter of keeping up with the local, national and world news. You'll also need to keep your eyes and ears finely tuned to spotting clues or signs of upcoming changes in the economy. Some of these will come not only from what you read in the newspapers but also from what you hear on the street and see for yourself.

As an example, I was recently waiting in a long checkout line at Costco. Standing directly behind me was a young businessman with one of those huge, heavy-duty carts filled with various supplies.

I asked him if he was in business locally and I learned from him that his businesses — a couple of day spas — were off by about one-third. He added that other fellow businessmen with whom he had been speaking reported similar declines.

Then, when I opened the newspaper the next day and read in the business section that sales and revenues were up, it gave me pause for thought. Can you always rely on what you read in the media?

Beware of the cheerleaders! Have you ever seen a real estate agent interviewed who didn't say that now is the best time to invest in real estate?

Or a stockbroker? Or someone selling cars or trucks?

You always want to be out in front of the others. Without superior knowledge of your subject or subjects, you can't accomplish that.

If you see something that you believe is going sour, don't wait until the floor drops out and everyone is trying to sell. Bail out when you can still salvage some of your investment.

And if everyone is rushing to cash in on the newest boom, it's already too late. Don't bite. Only the early birds will cash in while the followers will be left with the crumbs, if any remain.

Finally, keeping a step ahead of the crowd also entails tracking seemingly minor local developments. However, it's these local developments that can work to your advantage if you're prepared to act. Perhaps, the state plans to construct a highway bypass around your town or a new federal courthouse will be erected downtown soon. Or a major employer plans to set up a large plant in your area.

If you're operating several small businesses or services, you can apply to get in on the ground floor should any of your businesses meet the needs of one or more of the planned projects.

Between networking and keeping yourself informed otherwise, you can be the early bird who catches the worm.

10.

Consider a Move

Sometimes a move to another city or town can make you a winner.

Let's say you currently live in a high cost-of-living area such as New York, Boston or San Francisco. You've been laid off from a well-paying job and simply can't afford to keep up with the high cost of living where you are now.

For example, rents in Boston are three times as high as rents in Tucson where my wife and I live. Other living costs in Boston, for example, with a few exceptions, are also markedly higher.

If you find yourself in this situation, and your resources are dwindling, you might consider a move. If you also find yourself isolated from your friends and social milieu because of your fall in economic status or if you lack a strong support system where you live now, all the more reason to consider a move.

Basically, you'd be looking for a place where the economy is stronger than where you are now living and the cost of living — housing in particular — is lower.

When you consider a town or city where you might move, you need to take into account not only the cost of living and economic opportunities, but such issues as schools, climate, social and cultural activities and distance to the nearest airport. If possible, choose someplace where you'd have an improved support system, i.e., relatives or friends.

If you find such a place and decide to move, you'll markedly reduce your cost of living and no longer feel self-conscious about your drop in income and the inability to go places and do things with your current circle of friends and acquaintances. Let's face it, it can be embarrassing to have to say, "I'm sorry, we're busy and we can't do that this weekend," when you know that the party on the other end knows the truth. In a new environment you won't need to contend with that issue.

Following is a list of the eight best cities in which to live (from CNN/Money.com):

- Austin, Texas
- Virginia Beach, Virginia
- Houston, Texas
- Colorado Springs, Colorado
- San Antonio, Texas
- Nashville, Tennessee
- Raleigh/Durham, North Carolina
- Dallas/Fort Worth, Texas

The above list is simply a sampling. There are many locations where the quality of life is considered good and where unemployment is relatively low.

A move will require a substantial amount of research and likely a trip or two to view your choice first hand. You should vet locations using extreme caution and ask lots of questions. You might even want to visit the area for a couple weeks.

A major part of your vetting experience should be to establish knowledgeable contacts, i.e., individuals who have been around for a long time and can provide you with answers to questions that you might not find at the Chamber of Commerce or the usual places people go to gather information.

I've always preferred talking to a wise man or woman who knows a place from the inside and will tell me where to look and where not to look. The more of these individuals you can find, the more inside knowledge you'll have to help you make a decision.

If you reach that point where you're seriously considering a move and have decided on making an initial exploratory trip, consider booking a vacation rental online, a rental more comfortable and less expensive than a room at a hotel or motel, especially when you consider that you won't have to eat meals out. You'll be able to accommodate your entire family if necessary and save money that you'd spend at a lodging facility. My wife and I use Vacation Rental by Owner or one of the many other online websites for booking vacation rentals.

Before you make a final decision, it is advisable to make arrangements to return for a few weeks during which you can intensify your investigation, making further contacts and asking lots of questions.

If that subsequent trip meets all your criteria and you're comfortable with what you've seen and experienced, then it's time for a decision.

11.

Blend With the Locals

If you decide to move, it's important to waste no time in establishing yourself in your new community. That means making new friends and creating potential networking and business connections as soon as possible.

A key to this goal is connecting with organizations. I refer specifically to affinity groups which include hobbies, sports, the outdoors and other special interests. Also, consider affiliating with a church or a congregation of your choice. And there's yet one more way to connect — become a volunteer.

In most communities, volunteer opportunities abound. As examples, you can volunteer to tutor at a nearby school, help out at a food bank or staff a reception desk at a local hospital.

The point is to blend in and be considered a member of the community in the shortest possible time. You don't want to be viewed as an outsider for very long.

Some of the most successful independent business people I know are "joiners."

Speaking of blending in reminds me of an experience I had shortly after completing my graduate work in Wisconsin. I had returned to California after using my GI Bill for a later-in-life college education. I had job applications at a number of newspapers, but at the time no one was hiring.

Rather than sit at home and stare at the four blank walls of an apartment, I decided to register with several temp agencies. Within a day, I received a call back from one agency which sent me to a high tech company on a sprawling campus in Silicon Valley. I was to report at 8 a.m. to the company's maintenance foreman for assignment.

To blend in, I wore a blue chambray work shirt and a pair of jeans.

When I reported, the foreman consulted his to-do list and based on what was on his list he lined up his crew for the day, assigning me and an older hand, a regular full-time employee, to clean out some pigeon nests situated on a ledge of a two-story structure about 50 feet above ground level.

We had the use of what looked like an extended electric golf cart on which we carried an extension ladder along with other supplies.

When we arrived at the assigned location, the full-time employee, without speaking, gestured for me to help him remove the extension ladder from the cart and set it up.

Next, he handed me a special tool and some pigeon repellent to apply to the ledge after scraping it clean of pigeon nesting and droppings.

It was clear to me that due to his seniority he wanted me to ascend the ladder and that he would provide the needed ground support. I noticed, too, that he glanced at me suspiciously.

At the time, I was in my mid-thirties and quite agile. The job at the 50-foot level required no more than ten minutes, after which I descended the ladder. When back on the ground, I noticed that my co-worker was still eyeing me suspiciously, perhaps because he noticed that my hands weren't callused.

"Where did you learn to climb ladders like that?" he asked in a still-suspicious tone.

"In the Coast Guard," I replied without batting an eye.

That answer seemed to satisfy him and he was good company for the rest of the day. He even offered to buy me a beer after work.

That experience taught me a good lesson for the importance of blending in.

12.

Dual Citizenship?

If you or your spouse hold citizenship or dual citizenship in a foreign country, you might benefit from moving there.

This holds especially true for western European countries such as Norway, Denmark, Sweden, Germany, Austria, Switzerland, France or Holland.

In those countries, you'll usually find social services among the highest and the best in the world and considerably superior to those found in the U.S. Some other countries to add to your list are Canada, Australia and New Zealand.

If your foreign-born spouse has family ties in his or her home country, that's even more reason to consider moving there.

If you decide to make such a move, remember, there's no requirement that you must remain there.

My wife and I know of an American couple who moved to Switzerland more than 30 years ago to teach school. They enjoyed their work while prospering and are still there.

We also know an American woman who married a Scandinavian. She would have preferred to live in the U.S., but her husband can't find steady employment here. So, they remain in his home country where they live comfortably in a strong and stable economy with extraordinary social benefits, allowing them to travel to the U.S. and elsewhere whenever they wish.

13.

Is Senior Living for You?

If either you or your spouse is over 55, you can usually qualify for living in an age-restricted senior community.

Admittedly, "senior living" is not for everyone.

The key benefits are that senior communities are almost always well-maintained whether they're in a community of single-family houses, condos or mobile homes. Rules are strictly enforced and, generally speaking, residents are quiet and friendly. You won't have to put up with loud parties or racing motorcycles, etc.

If you buy or rent in a mobile home park, you usually can count on a very low expense compared to bricks and mortar residential properties.

Again, a senior community isn't for everyone, yet it's something to consider.

> **With the new day comes**
> **new strength and new thoughts.**
> ***– Eleanor Roosevelt***

14.

Handling More Bad News

Quite often, a layoff notice doesn't spell the end of bad news. Sometimes, there's more to come in the form of what one might call fallout. You should be prepared for these additional nuisances, and in my estimation that's exactly what they are — nuisances. They include being notified that your health insurance will be dropped in 60 days, that you'll no longer be eligible for club membership, etc.

These will prove to be trivial items once you take in the big picture. What you need to keep in mind first and foremost is that beginning now you're on the path to economic independence and no longer at the mercy of a single boss or a corporation. Granted, you might not be living at the same level as you were before, but you won't have to go to bed every night wondering if your job will be there for you tomorrow.

When I coached a Little League team in California and our kids were tagged out on a close call sliding into second base or home plate, we always prodded them to get up, dust themselves off and get back in the game to give it their best. Years later, as adults, these kids reflected those values which served them well.

You can do that, too.

Part II
How to Start Your Own Business

15.

Time is Money

An often-cited quotation of Abraham Lincoln is "A lawyer's time is his stock in trade."

This applies no less to you than it does to a lawyer.

You're no longer on the corporate or government payroll where your salary comes in rain or shine.

As I've noted earlier in this book, management of your time now takes on a much greater role in your life and may even affect your survival.

In the subsequent pages of this book, you'll encounter frequent references to time management and tips on how to come out on top.

To begin with, at all times you need to be thinking about rebuilding your financial fortress.

Also, as mentioned earlier, this begins with establishing a list of priorities on how you allocate your time. At the top of your list should be performance of actual work for money. That priority should trump all others. If a customer phones you on Saturday morning and asks if you can perform a service later that day, you drop anything else you're doing and fulfill the customer's request. Unless your house is on fire or you have a medical emergency, bringing income into the household is the most urgent priority.

Your second priority is *researching and planning* ways to earn money.

And at times when neither of these priorities are an issue, you might check on new ways to save money. Although there are many money-saving tips contained in this book, there are always new bargains and deals becoming available.

"How long am I going to have to do all this?" you might ask. Well, certainly until you have recovered from the trauma of losing a steady job and your finances are again stable.

However, most people who find themselves able to stay the course receive so much personal satisfaction from their triumphs that it becomes almost an obsession to continue to thrive and expand.

They'll tell you that every moment you spend playing electronic games, watching TV, surfing or texting is time *not spent* on the priorities that will make a difference in how you live in the years ahead.

You're likely familiar with the Vince Lombardi quote, "Winning isn't everything, it's the only thing." Well, for me, it's time management that is the *only thing*. Without it, there can be no successful control over your future.

> **What we really want to do is what we are really meant to do. When we do what we are meant to do, money comes to us, doors open for us, we feel useful, and the work we do feels like play to us.**
>
> ***– Julia Cameron***

16.

A Few Tips for Starting Up

Following is a list of essential Do's and Don'ts for anyone preparing to start their own business:

- **Don't borrow money or accept loans from *anyone*.** That includes the Small Business Administration (SBA), your bank, your credit card issuer, your uncle or your father-in-law. Businesses that start on borrowed money add an unnecessary extra obstacle to those problems that already exist. My approach has always been to start on a shoestring using your own capital, no matter how small an amount you have on hand. I've started many small business ventures; some have succeeded, many failed; but I've never borrowed a penny to start those businesses and never taken a loss that made an impact. Probably the greatest loss was the loss of my time invested.

- **Keep it simple.** If there's no special need to incorporate, either use just your own name for the business or adopt a DBA (Doing Business As), such as Jiffy Upholstery Cleaning or Desert Home Computer Services, etc. Some states require that you register the name. I believe what's most important is that you not choose a name that's already in use. If you find that you must limit your liability, you can register as an LLC (Limited Liability Company). You can do this yourself by purchasing a kit from a stationery store or online.

- **Read Jay Conrad Levinson's how-to books.** Although some were published several years ago, most of the information and tips are as valuable today as they were on their publication date. You can find used copies on betterworldbooks.com or abebooks.com (Better World provides free shipping and their prices are often lowest). Some of Levinson's best-known books are *555 Ways to Earn Extra Money* and his *Guerrilla Marketing* series. The first book will provide you with a wide range of choices for self-employment and, hopefully, inspire other ideas. The *Guerrilla* series provides tips for getting out the word about your business without needing to spend money on print or electronic advertising. Levinson is one of my heroes, and you'll be reading more in this book about how his strategies can help you. Meanwhile, here are a couple of bonus tips to add to the list of potential one-person independent businesses: Consider a new career as a mold detective/inspector or a house doctor. The latter performs house inspections and prepares reports for pending residential real estate transactions. Both jobs will require some training, though not an excessive amount of time. And remember, these or other jobs need not be your exclusive full-time occupation. You might need to have two or three skills in order to fill your work week.

- **Don't take in partners.** Only a small fraction of partnerships end well.

- **Don't try to raise money via crowd-funding** or similar vehicles.

- **Don't open an office.** Work from home. It's usually not prohibited in most cities and towns *unless* you have customers coming to your house in sizable numbers and it evokes complaints from your neighbors. Instead, arrange to go to your customers. Don't have them come to your house. Obviously, a business where customers and their vehicles come and go will be noticed by your neighbors and reported. Maintain a low profile and don't discuss your business with your neighbors if you can possibly avoid it. By working at home, I was able to offer very low prices to my customers. One day, while calling on the owner of a small high tech company in Silicon Valley for whom I produced a marketing newsletter, I was asked when I would be getting an office. My reply to the owner was, "When you're ready to help pay for it through an increase in my prices." He quickly reassured me that he was happy with the service and the low prices and that I need not trouble myself any further about getting an office.

- **Don't hire employees.** Outsource or subcontract anything that you can't do yourself. Also, recruit family members to pitch in if they're up to the task. Familiarize yourself with the IRS requirements to qualify as an independent contractor. This is important to avoid what I call a "gotcha." The IRS requirement standards are brief. Get a copy of these requirements and read carefully. Having regular employees opens a Pandora's box to more requirements than you can possibly imagine, far too many to enumerate here. Don't let yourself get caught in this quagmire.

- **Don't claim the home office deduction on your tax return**, even if you believe that you qualify. First, it raises a red flag on your return. I've been told this over and over again by tax preparers. If you don't claim the home office deduction, you can still deduct all other expenses connected with the operation of your business. This includes office and computer supplies, high-speed Internet connections, auto mileage and all other direct out-of-pocket expenses.

- **Strive to remain totally independent.** You'll have peace of mind, secure in the knowledge that there exists no one who holds the power to pull the economic rug out from under you. You're risking this when you allow your business to depend on a single large customer who could either switch his business to another independent provider or go belly up and leave you holding a huge bill which you'll never collect. Best to distribute the load. Think of your business and economic survival as a well-constructed cargo ship that's outfitted with about a hundred separate watertight compartments. If there's an accident, attack or fire, the vessel is all but unsinkable because only a few of the watertight compartments are affected and the ship can easily stay afloat with 80 or 90 percent of the compartments remaining watertight. Another way of saying this is don't put all your eggs in one basket.

- **Work out a business plan on your kitchen table.** It need not be fancy. It's only for use by you, but it helps you to remind yourself where you're headed. It's not to show to investors, bankers or venture capitalists. Steer clear of these folks. You don't need them.

- **Pay for everything when billed.** If you can't afford it today, don't buy it. Wait until you have the necessary funds in your checking account. To do otherwise will put you back on the hot seat. *Don't finance anything.* Never carry a balance. Resolve never to pay a penny in interest, late fees, service charges or the like. If financial institutions had to rely on what I've paid them in fees over the years, they would all have starved. The money I saved I invested and I'm still receiving returns on it today.

- **Be cautious in billing and extending credit.** When you feel you must extend credit, use my progress payment plan. It works like this: Explain to your customer before starting work that because you're small and independent you're unable to finance a customer's work. However, you compensate for that by offering lower prices.

  Then outline how you operate: (1) One-third of the total amount payable upon completion of the preliminary work. Of course, defining this depends on the nature of your business and is something that you'll need to calculate. (2) Payment of another third of the total amount after completing approximately two-thirds of the work. (3) Payment of the balance in 30 days following completion of the entire job.

This is a very fair approach for both vendor and customer. To hasten the customer's final payment you might decide to offer a two percent discount if the balance is paid within 10 days.

If a prospective customer hesitates at the start and offers some excuses why company policy won't allow them to make progress payments, my advice is to politely back off and suggest that they take their time to consider and contact you at a later time.

Don't waste any more time with them and don't call them in the future. If they call you, be extra, extra cautious. In more than 20 years in business, I believe only once or twice did I find a legitimate company to balk on agreeing to progress payments.

Once a customer has agreed to progress payments, you must stand firm in requiring that payment be received (not promise of a payment or "check is in the mail") before you resume work on the next phase or on a new project. You must hang tough on this and not be moved out of fear that the customer will drop you as a vendor. I can't remember a customer breaking off in mid-stream after they had already invested some of their money in the first or second phase. Bottom line: If you follow this procedure and stick to your guns, the most you can possibly stand to lose is the final third payment.

Should that occur, you can let the customer know that you'll be unable to continue with further work until that payment is received. If it appears to become uncollectible, don't waste your time and money hiring a lawyer. You'll be throwing good money after bad. Write it off, take a lesson from the experience and move on. You can't afford to dwell on it.

- **Build up your reserve cash for two purposes:** (1) You'll want to have instant access to funds dedicated exclusively to paying your vendors and subcontractors immediately.

  I was able to get better prices and excellent service from vendors and subcontractors with whom I worked because I treated each with respect and took an interest in their lives and because I immediately paid their bills. Actually, on the same day I received them.

  How did I manage this when I had to wait at least 30 days until my customers paid their balances? As my business gradually expanded, I realized that I'd need to find a way to pay my vendors promptly because many, like me, lived hand to mouth. I once had a meeting with a loan officer at my bank and quickly learned that what my dad had always said was true — that banks loan money only to those who don't need it.

  That might be a bit of an overstatement, but the end result was that despite my excellent credit record I didn't qualify for a line of credit.

  Consequently, I decided that I'd set money aside for the exclusive purpose of paying vendors and that since the banks wouldn't loan me money to bridge the gap between paying vendors and receiving payment from customers, I'd create my own bank, "The Bank of George."

  During the next six months I drastically reduced my already modest personal spending to a point where I purchased only absolute necessities.

  I hiked without cost with the Sierra Club on weekends and for entertainment I did a lot of late-night leisure reading at home. Within six months I had saved $5,000 which today, adjusted for inflation, might be triple or quadruple that figure. Thus "The Bank of George" was created, and I was able to expand my business while paying vendors immediately. I've included more details about this in Chapter 135.

Soon, I enjoyed a reputation among vendors as one of the few contractors who paid their bills upon receipt. But, the best benefit of all was that "The Bank of George" charged me no interest at all.

After that, yes, I did loosen the purse strings and took some dinners out with friends, saw some movies and relaxed a bit.

(2) The second purpose for stockpiling hard-earned cash is to get started buying residential income property. In my view, there's no better or more secure investment for the little guy than high-quality real estate. Later in this book, I'll elaborate on this issue.

**Where there is no work,
there is no dignity.**

– Pope Francis

17.

Specialty Businesses for Independents

Everyone, it seems, wants to work in a nice, clean company seated behind a large desk in an air-conditioned office with an expense account and two-hour lunches.

But, for most Americans, whether employed or self-employed, those days are gone forever.

Perhaps more important is this little secret: the dirtier and less glamorous the business — literally — the greater the chance of success.

My first exposure to this reality came some years ago after I'd moved into a house that required fix-up. Winter was approaching, and I could see that the furnace had not been serviced in a long time. When I inspected the furnace further, I noticed an old sticker pasted on an outside panel that bore the name of Gary's Furnace Cleaning Service along with a phone number. I called the number and found that indeed Gary was still in business. His appointment calendar was full for that month, but he worked me in for a later date and did a great job of bringing my furnace up to prime operating condition.

The above is an example of one of many specialty or niche businesses that dot our nation's economy. As one might expect, owners of such businesses don't go to bed at night worrying that Walmart or Costco might move into their town and put them out of business.

Another example is that of a middle-aged woman who, as a result of a divorce, became an owner of a tiny ceramics business. She had almost no knowledge of the business which had been started by her ex-husband. It was housed in a tiny, self-standing, roll-up unit in an industrial park with a garage-door-like entrance, a small work space, a tiny office and a toilet.

The business specialized in producing such items as soap dishes, toothbrush holders and toilet paper fixtures to match tiles in custom bathrooms. Most of her customers were interior designers who had bought and were about to install bathroom tiles for their customers, but found to their dismay — often at the last minute — that the tile companies couldn't furnish matching accessories such as those mentioned.

This woman's company would receive a sample tile from the interior designer, then custom manufacture the needed accessories in exactly the same color matching the already-purchased tiles.

When she took over the business, she operated with a single kiln and the help of one part-time employee. However, within months, bolstered by a marketing effort, her business took off. At the time I spoke with her, she reported having three kilns (the maximum number allowed due to limited space and electric power supply) operating 24/7 on three shifts.

Then there was a phone conversation I had with an enterprising woman who marketed kits online for repairing porcelain bathroom sinks and tubs. She got the idea for the kits as a result of her own success in commercially repairing sinks, tubs and ranges in her own home town.

She said that she'd been doing this type of work for several years and that during the housing boom of 2000-2008 she could barely keep up with the demand. Among her skills was also the ability to repair cracks in cultured marble tubs and showers. When one of these behemoths, complete with Jacuzzi, was delivered to a construction site and found to be cracked, she would immediately receive a call from an anxious contractor who, like others, couldn't afford the wait for replacement of the damaged tub. On receiving such a call, this woman said she would go directly to the construction site and within an hour or two repair the cracks to a level where they were completely undetectable. Often, she said, a fee for such an emergency service would range between $250 and $500, depending on the size and severity of the cracks.

According to the woman, her niche business ultimately enabled her to buy a strip mall shopping center.

Another woman I know started a home health care agency, operated it profitably for many years and recently sold it and retired very, very comfortably.

Besides niche businesses, there are many other types of businesses in which you'll dirty your hands, such as sewer and drain cleaning, janitorial services and collecting dog leavings from back yards of the affluent.

I remember once speaking to a man who owned and operated, with the help of a few employees, four sewer and drain cleaning trucks. He told me, "My friends kid me because I have an MBA and I do stinky work. And you know what? I tell them the money doesn't smell stinky when I deposit it in the bank."

Because many Americans disdain doing this type of work, which by the way pays very well, I passionately agree with those who conclude this about improving their chances for business success: "The dirtier, the better."

18.

The Benefits of Freedom

An assertion that I frequently hear coming from the self-employed is that working for yourself is demanding, but at the same time also liberating.

This is true simply because you're free to make your own decisions and use your time the way you want.

When I went off the weekly payroll and was left to fend for myself, I worked long hours, often without a day off for weeks at a time.

Because I could plan and control my schedule, when I wanted to do some personal things during the day, I shifted my workload to take care of business at home in the evenings.

I particularly remember one example of using such an opportunity. Back when I was employed, I'd come home at night and watch the evening news during dinner. About once a month, the local TV news would carry an item about a notable guest speaker appearing at a weekday luncheon of the Commonwealth Club in San Francisco, about 30 miles north of where I lived and worked. I had often thought about how enjoyable it would be to attend such an activity and hear someone speak in person who was a national newsmaker.

The opportunity finally came, when I started my own business. I found that for a very modest fee I could become a member of the Kenna Club at the University of Santa Clara, which was near to my home. The Kenna Club featured monthly guest speakers at their luncheons.

The featured speakers were a mix of domestic or internationally-known figures. It was fascinating to hear and see these newsmaker personalities who I'd previously seen only on TV.

Not only did I enjoy these events, but I sometimes invited my customers to join me as my guests.

When I returned home after these luncheons, I could do whatever catch-up was needed, a direct benefit of that personal freedom that you don't have on a job.

Another benefit of working for yourself is that even if your business sometimes requires repetitious activity, you don't get bored. Somehow, when you're doing a humdrum task for your *own* business, it's no longer boring. Every time you perform a monotonous job for one of your customers or ship an order, you know the task translates into money in your bank account.

I quickly became accustomed to this way of life, and despite the long hours, a team of draft horses couldn't have dragged me back to being under someone's thumb again.

I was more than happy to pay any price for this wonderful sense of freedom.

To which I would add, if you decide to follow this route: You cannot overestimate the value of independence and pride of ownership. It's *your* business, as small or modest as it may be, and no one can pink-slip you or take all your business away from you. Of course, there will be ups and downs, but it's still *your business.* You'll find deep intrinsic satisfaction on which you cannot place a price tag.

19.

If They're Not Nice...

You might be surprised to read this, but you should reject business from customers whose first impression tells you they aren't nice folks.

During my corporate life, I worked with and for some great people. Truly wonderful individuals. But, I also found myself working for a few real stinkers.

When I went independent, I told myself I'd never again work for anyone who wasn't fair-minded and considerate of others.

Believe it or not, over a twenty-year period I only once found myself confronted with this issue. A preferred customer of mine who was in the human resources department of a Silicon Valley corporation called and informed me that his counterpart at one of the company's affiliates needed someone to produce an employee newsletter, and that he'd recommended me.

I made an appointment to see this individual who turned out to be a very dislikeable and insensitive person. I couldn't imagine working for him, even for one day.

Not wishing to offend him or my customer who recommended me, I told him that I relied on subcontractor editors who I assigned and that I needed to check to see who might be available for a new assignment.

The next day, I phoned him and informed him that I had made numerous calls but couldn't find anyone available who would be appropriate for the task. I thanked him for having considered my company.

Bottom line: Don't agree to do work for anyone who you don't like or where you sense problems from the start. It's a safe bet that your intuition will prove to be correct.

20.

You'll Need a Website

Almost without exception, if you intend to be in business, you'll need a website. It need not be elaborate or large in scope. And you need not spend a lot of money. Perhaps, none at all, if you can manage that as some entrepreneurs do.

First, you need to make a list of what you believe needs to be posted on the website. If you look at other websites, you'll see that most have a home page, a list of products or services, an "About Us" page providing some details concerning the history of the company and its owner(s) and a "Contact Us" page.

As noted, there are some web hosting sites that are free. Use the Google Search and enter such words as "free website hosting" in the search box.

You can create your website without paying for a domain name which you might not necessarily require. Often you can ride on the wings of the website host who already has a domain name.

And you might also be able to avoid the expense of a web designer because now there are do-it-yourself templates for designing just about everything, including a standard website.

If you find that using the templates is a challenge, then consider checking with your friends to see if someone has a son or daughter with the skill to design a basic website for you.

Meanwhile, be sure to keep your website current. New phone? New email address? Place that information on your website immediately.

Whatever you decide, you don't need to spend more than a few hundred dollars on a website. Anything beyond that would be unnecessary and excessive.

Keep your costs low or, if possible, pay nothing.

21.

An Email Address is an Absolute Must

For those in business today an email address may be more widely used than a telephone number.

In addition to your website address, be sure to include your email address *and* phone number on your business cards, ads, invoices, statements, service orders, promotional mailings and anything else where your business name appears — both electronically and on paper.

You should maintain an email address solely for your business. Don't have business messages and inquiries coming to your personal email account. You can open free email accounts at Google, Yahoo and Microsoft's Hotmail, to name a few.

Perhaps, you'll find that the email screen name you want to use for your business email address is already taken, but you can surmount this obstacle either by varying the style or spelling of the name or more simply by just adding a couple of numbers at the end.

As an example, if you wanted to use the name *Bob'sPlumbing@yahoo.com* and find that it's already taken, it's a safe bet that *Bob'sPlumbing74@yahoo.com* is still available.

22.

How to Market Cheap (or for Free)

Some large businesses and institutions must advertise to maintain their revenue streams. They budget substantial amounts every year for both print and electronic advertising. These include new car dealers, grocery chains, furniture and discount appliance stores, etc.

Since your fledgling independent business likely doesn't fall into any of these categories, you can get away spending little or nothing to bring in new business and new customers.

Here's how it's done: First, *Craigslist* (www.craigslist.org) is the most widely used form of advertising for individuals and independent business folk. And it's free!

If you haven't had previous experience using *Craigslist*, get online now and spend some time checking it out. By looking at some of the examples you'll see where and how you can use this service to promote your business.

This might require developing some custom strategies. As an example, for several years, a woman I know co-chaired an annual flea market sale to benefit our neighborhood organization. For several weeks leading up to the day of the sale, she advertised some of the sale items on *Craigslist* and included color photos. She refreshed the ads frequently, which helped boost the total revenue of the flea market.

You should give this website careful study, since it's one of the most effective advertising tools around. And, of course, the price is right.

Next to using *Craigslist*, I strongly recommend that you obtain copies of Jay Conrad Levinson's books on *Guerrilla Marketing.* There are at least three or four different titles, some dealing with *Online Guerrilla Marketing* and others with the subject in general.

As the name implies, the objective of *Guerrilla Marketing* is to use whatever means possible to avoid having to pay for advertising or publicity. And believe me, there are few if any strategies that Levinson has overlooked.

His *Guerrilla Marketing* was named by *Time* as one of the top 25 business books with over 21 million copies sold.

In my opinion, there should be a statue erected in memory of this remarkable individual who died in 2013.

Before you go further, take a moment to read Levinson's profile in Wikipedia: www.wikipedia.org/wiki/Jay_Conrad_Levinson

Besides being available in hard copy on sites such as Amazon, BetterWorldBooks and Abebooks, you can also get ebook downloads of his books from Apple's iTunes.

Don't miss out on what this man has to say. His books have helped millions of folks around the world establish themselves in self-supporting small businesses.

Another possible strategy for bringing customer attention to your service or product is through social media. I've heard mixed results about this approach, and I can't say that I'm enthusiastic about it.

However, if you have a product that would appeal to a certain demographic, it might pay for you to arrange for a guru or a recognized expert in a specialty area within a particular social medium to tweet your product to his 12,000 followers.

I recently talked with such a guru who told me he reached out to thousands of followers on behalf of an author and his new book. And while he did get his message across, the resultant sales figures were abysmal.

So, at this time I'm skeptical of using social media to build your business.

Instead, I recommend sticking with *Craigslist* and Jay Conrad Levinson's tips. The latter will provide you with so many ideas for marketing your service or product that you can keep busy for years trying all of them.

What you shouldn't do, in my opinion, is pay to advertise online or in the newspaper or in any other print publication. The prices are all but prohibitive, and in my experience the ads have seldom if ever paid for themselves. If you feel you must pay to advertise, then test this approach by running a single ad and checking your results.

Direct mail or front door hand deliveries are among other methods for getting the word out. However, while both are more expensive than the strategies discussed above, under certain limited circumstances they might make economic sense.

One example would be if you are targeting a specific neighborhood to provide a service to, let's say, approximately 300 prospective homes. In such an instance, you might be better off printing flyers and paying someone to hand deliver them to each door. After all, why spend time or money to circulate your message among a much larger or broader area when it's not necessary.

Another instance would be if you want to reach all the property managers in your town or city. You could either rent or make up your own mailing list and send your mail piece to them exclusively.

Again, you can try these marketing strategies on a limited test basis without much risk.

23.

Phone? Don't Pay for a Business Listing

When you're starting out in business, it's essential to keep all your costs low. One way you can save money is to use your personal phone — landline or cellphone — as your business phone as well.

For this purpose I prefer a landline because it gets me a listing in the phone book and on all online directories. Also, when you phone a customer, your name will pop up on his caller ID. If you are calling him from your cellphone, in most instances only your telephone number and the name of the city from which you are calling will show up on the caller ID. There are exceptions to this, of course.

Some phone companies will allow residential customers to add a couple words after their names for a modest extra charge, such as *Walter Rogers, arborist.* If your local phone company permits that, you might wish to go for it because it provides you with the key advantage of a business listing at the cost of a residential listing plus a small added cost. If that option isn't available, go just with your name and/or address.

Another advantage of having a landline is that the phone company will usually offer unlimited domestic long-distance calling for a modest extra fee or as part of a bundle deal. This is important only if you are doing a lot of business with customers in different states and there are shipping questions, etc.

If for some reason, however, you find that it's necessary for your business to appear in the Yellow Pages with others in your area of specialty, then you have no choice but to go with a business telephone.

Again, your challenge is to keep costs down while still being accessible to your customers.

> **The way to wealth is as plain as the way to market. It depends chiefly on two words, industry and frugality: that is, waste neither time nor money, but make the best use of both. Without industry and frugality nothing will do, and with them everything.**
>
> ***– Benjamin Franklin***

24.

Keep a Low Profile

Although I touched on this in an earlier chapter, I can't sufficiently emphasize the importance, if you're operating a home-based business, of maintaining a low profile when it comes to your neighbors, homeowners association (HOA) or mobile home park management as well as city, county or state regulators.

Generally speaking, home-based businesses are not in violation of anyone's rules or ordinances so long as they are not seen or heard by their neighbors.

For example, there are millions of Americans today who telecommute their jobs from home. They use a computer and telephone in their work, but they disturb no one outside their home.

Even though you will not be functioning as a telecommute employee, you must also observe certain protocols or rules when it comes to your neighbors or homeowners association.

This means that you don't have customers or clients coming to your home. Instead, you go to their home or place of business.

Secondly, you don't have power saws or noisy equipment which could disturb your neighbors. If you do, you'll promptly get complaints likely followed by a formal notice to shut down.

Also, if you reside in a development whose homeowners association maintains strict regulations and you drive a vehicle with the name of your business painted on the side, you might want to park the vehicle inside your garage or carport where it can't be seen from the street.

You can be on the computer or the phone all day or all night and no one will notice or complain, but once your business activity is heard or observed outside your house, you invite problems.

That said, you'll also need to steer clear of the governmental factor. Some cities maintain strict licensing regulations. Some can also require inspections and follow-ups. For this reason, I recommend that you don't get into any kind of business in which you're selling food. If you do, it's a guarantee that you'll have to deal with ongoing red tape and heavy-duty regulations, requirements and inspections.

As for city, county and state regulators, if you're in a business that requires you to collect sales tax, you must apply for a sales tax license. However, when you do so, be careful not to overstate your expected business volume or you might be asked to pay a larger deposit.

Also, keep in mind that if you must register your business, the unincorporated areas of the county generally have less strict policies and ordinances than cities. If you have an option to use an address in the unincorporated area, you'll most often be subjected to fewer headaches than if you hold a city license. And the fees for a county license are also often lower.

You'll also find that once you've registered with almost any local or state government office, you'll soon be besieged with mail and forms from every conceivable agency with questions asking about the number of people you employ, the value of your inventory, etc.

Your response should be that you have no employees and that you have no inventory, if that is the case. Respond immediately to all inquiries or the agencies will continue to badger you.

Ultimately, forms to fill out and other similar requests for information will cease, but meanwhile be prepared.

As for Uncle Sam, I make it a policy to report every penny of income to the IRS. Just be sure to keep track of all your business-related expenses and play everything straight up. The IRS is interested only in collecting taxes. They have no interest in whether you are a home-based business or meet local requirements, etc.

25.

Ten Best States for Entrepreneurs

For those considering a move, you might take notice of a list recently posted on CNN.Money/com which ranks in order the ten best states for starting a new business.

Of course, there are many other factors to consider when moving and this is just a single index to enter into the mix.

Also please understand, I'm not urging or encouraging anyone to move.

When perusing this list, you need to keep in mind the cost of living differentials. It's a fact for example that the square foot cost of a house or condo in Manhattan is *ten times* the cost of a comparable unit in Tucson, Arizona.

Although rents and food costs might not be *ten times*, they're significantly higher as are most of the other costs of living.

So, if you're currently living in a high-cost area and it becomes apparent that you won't soon be getting hired at a job with a salary that you previously earned, you might consider reestablishing yourself in an area with a lower cost of living.

Following is the CNN list of best states for new businesses:

1. Montana
2. Vermont
3. New Mexico
4. Alaska
5. Mississippi
6. California
7. Idaho
8. Hawaii
9. Louisiana
10. Nevada

26.

Surprise Source of Extra Income

If you have an extra bedroom in your house or apartment that you're not using, consider renting it.

What's critical in doing this is to screen ultra-carefully and rent only to a single person. Having one individual underfoot in your house is likely as much as you or your family could comfortably tolerate.

Renting a room in your house means establishing a number of requirements the applicant must meet.

The first step in this process is that when you advertise your vacancy, whether on Craigslist, the local newspaper or on a bulletin board in the neighborhood Laundromat that you include the words "non-smoking." This is assuming, of course, that there are no smokers in your family. Fair housing laws in most states won't permit you to say "no smokers" since that's viewed as discriminatory because a smoker can respond saying, "look I'm agreeable to not smoking inside your house." However, in most states "non-smoking" is acceptable and you can require that no one smoke in your house.

You can also include the words "references required" and "credit check."

Your next step is to set up a special outgoing message on either a voicemail or answering machine. This might require a bit of juggling if you have only one phone. If you or your spouse has a second phone number and you can devote it exclusively to screening calls for a few days, you'll be able to separate your personal or business calls from the room rental venture. This step is a critical part of the screening.

In your outgoing message, describe the room that's available and whatever facilities or household privileges are included. You also need to lay down minimum requirements, including references from previous landlords and proof of an *excellent* credit record. Yes, you read that right — *excellent.* Not good or just okay, but *excellent.*

A credit record is perhaps one of the best predictors of all aspects of behavior. If the applicant has a long record of paying his or her bills on time, it's likely that he or she will pay you on time, too. It's also an indication that this person manages their affairs well.

In your outgoing message, you also say that loud stereos or waterbeds are prohibited and that you're seeking an individual who is considerate of others who are sharing space with them in the house.

Finally, request that the caller leave his or her *first* and *last* name and a phone number where they can be reached.

If the person doesn't leave a last name, it's an indication that they aren't likely to follow any of your rules, so in my opinion, no need to phone them back. They failed to follow your instructions.

When you do contact them via phone, you might say that you'd like to answer any questions they might have, and of course you'll have questions that you'd like to ask them.

While you shouldn't hesitate to ask important questions, you must be careful not to ask any questions that might be considered discriminatory, such as those touching on race, religion, gender, age, or sexual orientation.

You should also point out any limitations about the room for rent, such as availability of parking and other amenities that may or may not be available.

If you reach the end of your conversation and find that you and the prospective tenant might be a match, only then arrange for an on-site showing.

At the same time, ask the prospective tenant to bring along a recent copy of their credit report. Applicants can download these at no cost once a year from any of the three major credit reporting agencies, whereas you can't do it for them, even if they request it. For a landlord to obtain a credit report nowadays is more difficult than pulling teeth. However, it can be done, but be prepared to jump through a number of hoops.

If the credit report tells you that the individual has an excellent credit record, then hand him or her an application which you can download for free from the Internet.

And if that goes okay, you can provide him or her with a lease to sign. You can download sample leases from the Internet and customize them to suit your circumstances.

If the applicant has trouble coming up with the first week's or month's rent plus the security deposit, this isn't a good sign and it's unlikely that you'll be receiving rent payments on time.

If you wish to take a further step to ensure prompt payment, you can include a provision in your lease saying that rent paid on or before the due date is entitled to a five percent discount. Renters love that clause.

Because you are requiring that applicants have an excellent credit history, don't expect your phone to ring off the hook. Only somewhere between 10 and 20 percent of Americans have an excellent credit rating. That means that about four out of five people who see your ad will pass over it and continue searching because they know that they couldn't qualify.

Finally, as another source of income, if you live in a condo or apartment in a high-density area where parking spaces are at a premium, and you don't have a car but have a reserved parking space, you can rent it out for a substantial amount. In Manhattan or in Boston, for example, an enclosed parking space can rent for several hundred dollars a month.

27.

If in Doubt, Deduct

When you start a business, you might be surprised to learn that your income is not only taxed by the federal government and often the state in which you reside, but that you're also liable for a combined federal self-employment tax (which includes Social Security and Medicare) of approximately 15 percent.

In the past, it's likely that you and your employer shared the cost of this 15 percent tax, often referred to on printed statements as FICA or Federal Insurance Contributions Act.

When you begin to add a 15 percent self-employment tax to let's say a 15 percent federal income tax and a two percent state income tax, you are paying almost a third of your modest income in taxes.

Admittedly, this is a back breaker if not an entire deal breaker. And it's discouraging to face something like this from the very start.

However, if you're willing to make some major changes in your money management decisions and lifestyle, there are remedies.

The government allows you to decrease your taxable income by deducting certain business-related expenses. All or most of these expenses are what is known in accounting lingo as "above-the-line deductions." These deductions come directly off your business income and aren't subject to treatment given other deductions that qualify only if they exceed your gross adjusted income (AGI) or meet certain other requirements. In plain English, they are the most preferred of all deductions.

However, and this is an important *however*, you must be able to substantiate — if audited by the IRS — that these are legitimate deductions for genuine business-related purposes.

What is a legitimate deduction? Well, if you use money from your business to take a vacation trip to Hawaii with your family or buy new furniture for your living room, you clearly cannot consider these deductible expenses.

But if you provide fully-paid health care coverage to your sole employee, such as your spouse, and the plan also covers his or her dependents (including yourself), such an expense is deductible. This kind of deduction is covered in detail in Chapter 33.

So, if you concentrate on allocating as much as you can of your initially modest business income toward legitimately deductible business-related expenses that also benefit you and your family, such as a health care package, you will be able to substantially bring down your combined tax bill (federal and state income taxes and Social Security). This is by no means an easy chore and requires long range planning plus the ability to put off buying items for personal use that aren't business deductible.

A tax lawyer I knew often advised, "If in doubt, deduct."

This doesn't mean that you should try to deduct obvious personal expenses, but if you can adequately defend your deduction were you to be audited, then deduct.

Here's a good example: You buy a new desktop computer for your business. It's a must, and you have a dozen good reasons why you can't operate your business without it. However, you and your spouse occasionally use the computer to check personal email and your kids sometimes play video games on it when you're not using it for business.

If you're audited, you might be asked questions about who uses the computer and when. If so, you should be prepared to answer.

Ordinarily, an IRS auditor isn't going to waste time delving into petty issues. But suppose that he did so. The worst possible outcome would be that the agent doesn't allow you to deduct 100 percent of the computer cost as a business-related expense and that you're liable for income tax on let's say one-third of the cost of the computer because he's determined that's the estimated percentage of personal use.

When the IRS selects tax returns for audit, it's usually looking to catch big fish and collect big unpaid taxes. So, as long as you avoid claiming unsupported business expenses and stick to deducting only those expenses that you can confidently explain, you'll provide yourself a tax advantage and have no fear of any close scrutiny of your tax return.

An excellent aid for guiding you in this area is *How to Maximize Schedule C Deductions & Cut Your Self-Employment Taxes to the Bone — What Your Accountant Will Never Tell You* by Barbara Brabec. It's available in ebook format from Amazon. If you don't own a Kindle, Amazon will provide you with a free software download to enable you to read or print out the book on your desktop computer.

Later in this book, you'll find a chapter on rental income property. This type of investment comes with significant tax write-offs due to depreciation. If you bring your business to the stage where you're able to someday acquire and manage your own rental property, you'll gain significant tax benefits together with additional economic security. You should look into this option at the appropriate time.

28.

Avoid Express Delivery Costs

Everyone knows what it is to race against a deadline. When white-knuckle time arrives, we rush either to the fax machine or to a form of express delivery.

Express delivery can be costly. A $30 or $40 charge for overnight delivery isn't uncommon. And you'll likely pay in the low $20 range for second or third day delivery.

Regardless of whether you opt for express delivery using FedEx or UPS or the U.S. Postal Service, you can figure on a hefty charge.

In my view, this is a huge waste of money and is totally unnecessary.

I know some independent business folks who spend a couple hundred dollars a week on express delivery when they could avoid this expense.

Can you afford to toss away a couple hundred dollars a week? I sure can't.

If your customer is late and asks you to ship to him via express delivery, that's one thing. It's not coming out of your pocket.

But if things are running late because of your failure, then you need to do something about it. Now. And here's how.

You meet deadlines without stress by inserting a time cushion into any project that has a firm deadline date.

You do that in several ways. First, always allow for the possibility that something is going to pop up in your life or someone you're counting on will cause a delay. With a built-in cushion, you can accommodate the delay and still make your deadline.

Now, here's the trick. If you're working with a deadline — even if it seems that you have plenty of time — don't tell a tradesman or repair person that you're not in a hurry. Never. When I'm working with a sub-contractor, I never reveal my customer's *actual* deadline. If the work needs to be completed and in my hands no later than May 1, I tell him that my customer needs the work completed no later than April 27. Using this cushion, I've never missed a deadline.

When my wife and I travel, I always set my deadline for having all packing and other arrangements completed at least one day before our actual departure. And guess what? There's never any spare time left. Something always pops up at the last minute. That's when a time cushion saves us again.

I've been in business for myself for more than 30 years and I can't recall paying an express delivery charge out of my own pocket more than once or twice. I've taken many envelopes and packages to FedEx over the years, and have received even more, but almost always these express delivery shipments were paid for by someone else. Not me.

> **Lost time is never found again.**
>
> ***– Benjamin Franklin***

29.

Inside Sources

While all sources of relevant information are helpful, inside sources are invaluable.

An example is the case of a couple I know who transported the wife's ailing and aged mother to Arizona from another country on a visitor's visa. Due to the mother's condition, they had no time to wait months in applying for and waiting to receive a regular visa.

When the mother's visitor's visa expired, the couple received a letter from the immigration service notifying them that the 88-year-old woman must return to her homeland.

The problem was that although the couple was willing to assume all responsibility for the mother's care, there remained no one in her homeland to take care of her.

After the couple received a second letter from immigration officials warning that deportation proceedings would follow, they contacted a young immigration lawyer who informed them that a court appeal was an expensive process with little chance of success. However, if they wished, he would proceed upon receipt of a $10,000 advance retainer payment.

They were desperate and contacted me for help. I arranged for a consultation with a more experienced immigration lawyer with whom I was acquainted. She carefully examined the documents, then advised us that bringing the case to court was almost certain to fail and that the expense would be a waste.

However, she confided to us that her sources had informed her earlier that the office in California from where the computer-generated correspondence originated was inundated with such cases and was grossly understaffed.

She said she'd also been informed that the basement in that particular government office was filled with carton after carton of similar cases which could not possibly be brought to court or enforced any time in the near future, given the staff shortage. She recommended no action for the time being and suggested that everyone just sit tight.

Five years later, still in this country, the wife's mother died peacefully of natural causes. The attorney is also now deceased. Now, fifteen years later, the couple still hasn't received any further contact from the authorities.

Another example was the time I sought to move from working at a smaller newspaper to a larger one. I knew a reporter who worked on the larger newspaper and invited him to lunch, informing him in advance that I wanted to ask him some key questions and seek his suggestions.

Among other advice offered, he came up with this gem: The executive editor who did the hiring had never hired an applicant who didn't come back to see him at least *three times*. I suppose the rationale was that if an applicant really wanted the job he'd put forth this kind of an effort.

I followed his advice and within a couple weeks following my third visit, I received a phone call asking if I'd be willing to start by working a *Sundays only* late night shift. Within a couple months I was moved to a temporary 40-hour work week which after six months became permanent.

I could fill this book with stories like this. Suffice it to say that whenever you can get the jump on a situation by having an inside source, you will most likely benefit significantly.

How do you develop these sources? By being an outgoing individual and supporting friends and acquaintances. Do your networking and also keep your contact information up to date.

When you need to know what's going on inside a company or government office, contact one or more of your resources who might have access or can possibly put you in touch with someone who does.

30.

Capital Preservation

You likely won't get this advice from others, but I take a contrarian view when it comes to the subject of borrowing money. Don't — for *any* purpose. No matter what. Ever.

Borrowing money destroys your independence. You'll always have an obligation hanging over your head. A payment is due. And another. And then another. You'll pay more for everything because the real price also includes the interest you must pay.

My wife and I have been debt-free for more than 25 years. We don't owe anyone. We drive cars that are more than 30 years old. We don't try to keep up with the Joneses. The Joneses might have a mortgage on their house, a loan on their new SUV and ulcers from worrying about how to keep their lives together.

We're independent, and we love living this way. What's more, we both sleep well.

To advance to this financial position does, however, require some sacrifice and self-discipline.

In Chapter 16, Tips for Starting Your Business, I noted how I created the Bank of George in order to have the needed cash on hand to pay vendors and accommodate modest expansion, etc. Further details are provided in Chapter 135.

If you can create your own Bank of Sam or Bank of Susan, you'll find yourself sleeping better as well as saving significant amounts of money you might have wasted on loan interest.

Capital preservation also requires that you have sufficient cash on hand to handle emergencies and unexpected expenses such as repairs or medical costs.

Almost every day I have occasion to swallow hard and keep from commenting when I see acquaintances using their credit cards to buy useless junk or pay for extravagant weddings or expensive trips. They'll be paying for their poor judgment calls for years to come at rates of anywhere from 18 to 24 percent and sometimes higher.

Even worse are those who borrow cash on their credit cards and obligate themselves to pay cash fees plus an exorbitant interest rate.

As I mention elsewhere in this book, you should use your credit card only to buy what you truly need and be prepared to pay your credit card bill in full when it arrives.

Meanwhile, stockpile all the cash you can and hold on to it for those rainy days because — trust me — those rains or even storms are sure to come.

When some state and city governments encountered severe budget problems a few years ago and in some cases even went into bankruptcy, a neighbor who is a retired accountant asked, "Didn't those governments ever expect that there would be a rainy day?"

Did I? Did you?

> **Nobody ever drowned in his own sweat.**
>
> ***– Ann Landers***

31.

Hire Your Spouse and Kids

If you've started your own business, and some money is coming in, you can hire your wife and kids to help reduce your tax liability.

There are many benefits to employing your immediate family members, including a major advantage, that being how you provide health care coverage. This is detailed separately in Chapter 33.

Because tax codes and regulations are constantly changing and the requirements vary from state to state, you'll need to consult with your accountant or tax advisor for details. Do it before you make a move. It will be worth your time and will keep you out of trouble with the IRS.

> **Our greatest weakness lies in giving up.**
> **The most certain way to succeed is**
> **always to try just one more time.**
>
> ***– Thomas A. Edison***

32.

Using PayPal

You may have customers who wish to pay you using VISA, but don't try to set up a VISA account with your bank unless you are processing hundreds of charges per month. The banks will charge you between two and four percent of the sale amount plus monthly fees plus a substantial amount for equipment. You might also require a dedicated phone line, leading to yet more equipment and expense. Instead, accept VISA payments via PayPal. There are no upfront costs and whatever the percentage of sale they charge, it's a bargain when you compare it with the alternative. You'll find that many home-based businesses use PayPal for all their credit card transactions.

> **You have to learn the rules of the game. And then you have to play better than anyone else.**
>
> ***– Albert Einstein***

33.

Health Care Bonanza

I picked up this little gem from a friend who works at a full-time job, but owns a small home-based business on the side.

Before describing how he has set this up, I'll note two important caveats: (1) In order to implement his plan your business needs to have reached the point where you have sufficient money coming in the door to pay for it; and (2) You'll need to check extra-carefully with your accountant or a trusted and qualified tax advisor as to whether it still holds or if there have meanwhile been changes in the tax code that won't allow you to do this. I urge you to proceed *very* carefully because you don't want to implement this plan and then later at tax time encounter a "gotcha." Remember, on important moves it's critical that you consult experts and ask enough questions to ensure that you're on very solid ground.

Here's what my friend does: He hires his wife as the sole employee of his sideline business and pays her a modest salary.

As his sole employee, he provides her with 100 percent, fully-paid health care coverage for herself and also for her spouse (that's him) and their dependents (the kids).

Because his wife, as an employee, provides legitimate services to his business as an employee, his business' health care cost is deductible in its entirety from the very top of the income tax form. With this deduction, he not only avoids federal and state income taxes, but also self-employment tax (Social Security and Medicare tax).

However, the benefits accruing to his business don't end there. He also provides his sole employee (his wife), and of course her family, with a package that includes reimbursement for all uncovered medical expenses and co-payments as well as anything else that isn't covered by the basic health insurance plan.

In addition, he provides dental care insurance for her and her spouse and dependents and reimburses them for any dental expenses that aren't covered by the insurance. Yes, that's for the whole family.

And the package also provides reimbursement for all prescription drugs for the entire family.

Needless to say, this is an expensive health care package. Though until recently it's been fully deductible as a business expense, you'll need to have sufficient income from your business to pay for this plan as well as provide your spouse with a modest salary.

Keep in mind that the tax code requires that you provide *this same* health care plan — no changes or exceptions allowed — to any other employee that you hire. So before hiring an employee, other than your wife or kids, consider this requirement.

This, of course, is a good reason to have only one employee, that being your spouse.

However, this in no way prevents you from outsourcing services that you need should your business require it.

Regardless of your politics, simple good business practice calls for looking into the requirements and possible benefits of the Affordable Care Act. It could save you money and it also could help you avoid paying a penalty if you're not in compliance.

Again, you don't want to make a mistake on this one. Because there have been so many changes in the laws affecting health care and its tax impact, and very likely more to come, it is vitally necessary that you consult an expert, such as an accountant or tax lawyer, and then consult one more time. Make certain that your plan meets all state and federal requirements and that the professional who is providing you with advice is knowledgeable and up to date on the specifics of this issue. There are many accountants and advisors who are not up to date on this issue, sometimes because it's not an area in which their regular clients find themselves.

Recently, Congress has taken a close-up look at what has been referred to as Cadillac health care plans, such as that described here, and there have been proposals to place restrictions or a cap on these. Other pending legislation calls for yet more restrictions on these non-taxable benefits. However, a tax newsletter recently reported that under some new rules or proposed legislation, businesses with only one employee could claim a tax credit *not* simply a tax deduction for amounts spent on employee health care. This is a complicated issue subject to ongoing changes. Before taking any steps to implement a health care plan for your family and your business, it's imperative that you are in possession of all up-to-the-minute facts and rely *only* on the word of an expert or experts in this field. This is not only important. It is critical. Please take heed of this caution!

Note: In another part of this book I advise not having any employees when you start your business. This enables you when filling out forms to honestly state that you have no employees. Doing so will cut down on the amount of forms you'll be sent by various government agencies each month or quarterly. If you later decide to place your spouse on the payroll when you have adequate income to pay for the health care plan, you'll have been completely forthright because he/she was *not* an employee at the time you started the business.

34.

A Part-time Job for You?

You might not be aware that in recent years three-quarters of all newly-created jobs are part-time.

Consider this: There are three basic types of part-time employment. First, there's seasonal employment where you know exactly how long you'll be working. It's all up front and there are usually no surprises.

Then, there's so-called permanent employment by large corporations and also some smaller ones where you're given a work schedule of usually 30 hours a week or less. The company might have up to 90 percent of its work force working just under the limit for what's considered part-time (30 hours or less). This way they don't have to pay their employees any benefits including health insurance. There is usually little or no opportunity for advancement and the pay is usually poor.

The third type is temporary employment where both large companies and small businesses hire part-time or full-time workers to fill a gap. On occasion, they'll hire someone on a temporary or part-time basis in order to check out a prospective full-time worker. This way, if the employee doesn't work out to the management's satisfaction, they need not fire him. It you show them your best work under these circumstances, you have an excellent opportunity of landing a full-time job.

A recent study showed that employers now tend to hold older workers in high regard because of their experience and reliability. Although the type of work and pay level might not be equal to what you had in the past, you should consider such an opportunity simply because nothing better might come along, especially given that jobs are scarce. Even those that don't pay well.

I must emphasize, however, that in my view landing a low-paying job, even if it's full-time and permanent, shouldn't be your ultimate goal.

If it were me, and my own startup business wasn't yet bringing in enough to cover my basic expenses, I'd take the offered job and work hard to keep it *until* — and that word *until* is very important — I could get my own business up to the point where it would support my household.

It might even take a couple years of working nights and weekends on my own business to reach that point. However, in the meantime I'd be bringing in a paycheck that would cover my essential needs.

Optimism is the faith that leads to achievement. Nothing can be done without hope and confidence.

– Helen Keller

35.

Do You Take "No" for an Answer?

When I was working on a newspaper, I once received a letter from a community activist thanking me for chasing down a hard-to-get story.

In his letter, the man wrote: "George, you give meaning to the word *perseverance*."

I kept that letter, and at times when it seems that all doors are closed to me in a particular endeavor, I pull out that letter, read it over and receive a swell of inspiration to try again.

As a rule, if something you want is important enough, then it's worth putting out maximum effort and saying to yourself, "I'm not going to take 'no' for an answer."

Okay, so then what? First, what you *don't* do is repeat the steps you've already taken. You already know that those approaches have failed.

Now is the time to call on your best friends and smartest advisors. Tell them the necessary details and note that, figuratively speaking, you've already tried entering through the front door, but found it barricaded.

Might they have any suggestions for approaching through the back door or the side door or via the roof or basement? Again, of course, figuratively speaking.

Do they know anyone who might help you get in to see whoever it is you can't get in to see? Might they have a friend or a friend of a friend who is familiar with someone inside the company or organization?

Perhaps, you'll ultimately get in to talk with this important person and find that he or she will turn down your request, whatever it might be.

If that occurs and if you want to establish a relationship with that company at all costs, you might respond like this: "Ms. Jones, my long-time aspiration has been to serve your company. Would you allow me to provide you with a month of free service? It will be on me. That's how determined I am to show you that I can do the job your company needs. I'll do it better and at lower cost. If after the first month, you find that I 'pack the gear,' then I'll be pleased to quote you a price that's extremely competitive. If I don't pass the test, I pick up my equipment and tiptoe out the door with no fuss or bother. Would you consider this?"

Obviously, not everyone who receives this offer will accept it. But, I see it as the last effort in a long line of attempts to get the business. What's to lose?

Another approach, particularly if you happen to be seeking employment, is to make regular visits to the hiring person where you've applied. (A reference to this technique is mentioned in Chapter 29.) You must keep your visits brief, very brief and be sure not to disrupt any work activity that might be going on. The prime purpose is simply to let the hiring person know that you're very interested in the job, but you don't want to make a nuisance of yourself. The rationale here is that those who hire would prefer to employ someone who really wants to work there rather than have to phone applicants who might have already found another job.

This approach is often counterproductive if you're a business owner and have already made a presentation to the decision makers. Contacting them regularly with follow-up calls or visits is usually not effective and can alienate them. Save this technique for use only if you're seeking employment.

36.

Commute "Smart"

A major part of efficient time management is avoiding long commutes.

If you're in business for yourself, your time is what you have to sell. Frittering it away or burning it up in bumper-to-bumper commutes is like flushing fifty-dollar bills down the toilet.

If you're serving customers in a particular area, it pays to reside as near to that location as you can.

Keep this in mind when you're searching to rent or buy a place to live.

Doing that will make it very convenient for you and save travel time as well. But, what about serving those customers who are located long distances from where you live, often outside the city limits?

I know of several independent service providers who impose either an added trip charge or fuel surcharge for service calls that are long distances from their home base. And given the cost of gasoline, such a policy seems entirely reasonable.

However, there are exceptions. Suppose you have a steady customer whose facility lies 20 miles from your home and the company ranks among your best; in that case, you might want to reconsider imposing such a charge. There's a saying, "One size doesn't fit all," and I believe it applies here. (See also Chapter 81, "Beating the Traffic.")

Obviously, too, there's a difference if you impose a trip charge on a customer for whom you are performing a one-time troubleshoot on their computer as opposed to a manufacturer to whom you are supplying widgets by the gross every week. You wouldn't even want to mention a trip charge to the latter.

These same considerations also apply to the personal use of your vehicle. Obviously, making a 45-minute drive to the supermarket to buy a stick of butter constitutes a monumental waste of your time.

Stock up when you go shopping and avoid unnecessary trips and rush-hour traffic.

> **A business has to be involving,**
> **it has to be fun, and it has to exercise**
> **your creative instincts.**
>
> ***– Richard Branson***

37.

Beware of "Work-at-Home" Come-ons

One of the best sources for work at home is available on Clark Howard's *Work from Home Guide* found on his website www.clarkhoward.com

As noted elsewhere, when you consider "work from home" you must be aware that there are vast numbers of scammers, predators and exploiters waiting for an easy mark.

According to "America Now News," 2.8 million people fall victim to this scam each year.

In 2014, a federal judge in California fined a company $25.4 million for misleading more than 100,000 individuals who bought into a work-at-home offer.

First rule: If anyone ever asks you for money, even a nominal amount, cut the connection *immediately*. No good can come of it. Although that's a prime disqualifier, there are thousands who nevertheless will fall victim every year. Make sure that you're not one of them.

Then there are different exploiters. There are the exploiters who will try to get you to work for what comes out as less than the minimum wage or slave wages. That's if you are fortunate enough to get paid at all. Watch out for these.

However, there are some fairly good work-from-home, part-time jobs that are similar to work you would perform at a call center, such as taking reservations, quoting information, etc. When you come across what appears to be such an opportunity, you must carefully, and I repeat, *carefully* vet the offer.

Begin with a Google search of the company which is directly hiring you. You might be taking calls for a Fortune 500 company but are being hired by an intermediary, usually a contractor who is responsible for paying you for your time. Check out that entity, *not* the Fortune 500 company. Again, if they ask you to buy equipment or advance money for anything, drop them immediately.

Finally, if you do start the work and you aren't paid promptly after a week's work, inform the employer that you can't afford to extend them credit, that your own expenses must be met weekly and that you'll be pleased to resume work when you've been paid. Don't let anyone owe you for sums that you can't afford to lose. You should be able to discern if you're being given the run-around or if the employer is sincere about needing to delay payment for a few days because their payroll must first go through X, Y or Z channel.

Many individuals are intimidated and believe that if they're too direct in asking for their wages that they'll lose the job. Unfortunately, I know of too many cases in which this occurred and in the end the employee was owed five or six weeks pay, and never collected a penny.

Meanwhile, keep working on your own business during hours that you aren't engaged in the work-at-home job. It will be your own business that sustains you over the long haul and provides an income stream that can't be cut off by a single company or individual.

38.

Get-Rich-Quick Seminars

Don't waste your time attending get-rich-quick seminars or multi-level marketing pitches. Most are without merit, and the only person who gets rich is the promoter.

You can lose thousands of dollars if you allow yourself to be pulled in by the lure of easy money and a fast track to wealth.

Instead, concentrate on your own small, home-based business where you answer to no one except yourself.

> **The dictionary is the only place that success comes before work. Work is the key to success, and hard work can help you accomplish anything.**
>
> ***– Vince Lombardi***

39.

Social Security and Medicare

I consider this one of the most important chapters in this book. Don't skip it.

Many of you are already in your forties or fifties. Now is the time to check with Social Security to determine how many Social Security quarters you have to your credit.

Until recently, anyone wishing to draw on their Social Security has been required to have worked for a minimum of 40 calendar year quarters at a job where Social Security taxes have been withheld. Or if self-employed, to have paid in self-employment tax toward the accumulation of the needed 40 quarters.

There are a lot of details and fine print that accompany these basic rules, and you should know them, including the minimum age at which you can retire and how much you're allowed to earn without penalty after starting to draw payments.

Also of major importance is knowing what you'll need to qualify to receive Medicare which is usually available at age 65.

The minimum retirement age has been pushed up in recent years along with other changes.

So, if you haven't done so already, be sure to check current requirements online, by phone or by visiting your nearest Social Security office.

If you don't already have those 40 quarters accumulated, you should be sure to pay in at least the minimum required to qualify for every earned quarter even if you're exempt from paying federal income tax due to low income. Talk to your accountant on how you can do this. It's critical that you accumulate the required number of quarters so that you'll be eligible for both Medicare and

Social Security payments when you reach retirement age. Don't let this slip past you. Investigate thoroughly and without delay.

If you find that economic conditions are tough today, imagine living into your sixties, seventies or eighties without either Social Security or Medicare.

> **Ideals are like stars; you will not succeed in touching them with your hands. But like the seafaring man on the desert of waters, you choose them as your guides, and following them you will reach your destiny.**
>
> ***– Carl Schurz***

40.

Searching for New Income Sources

You'll find that Google and other search engines are a good source for helping you to earn money without a job.

Simply enter these words: "How to earn money without a job."

You'll be surprised at what might pop up.

For example, a small business idea that's working for someone in another state could very well be an idea that you can employ in your own locale.

Remember, you can never be exposed to too many ideas.

In the best case scenario, you'll find links to some very useful websites or affinity groups. However, many others are fraught with risk. Be careful!

> **What you get by achieving your goals is not as important as what you become by achieving your goals.**
>
> ***– Zig Ziglar***

41.

Skip Eating Out

Skip lunches and dinners out. If on certain occasions you can't eat at home, where the cost of your meal is usually half to one-fourth the price of a restaurant or fast food meal, then brown-bag it.

If you're out on one of your service calls for your business, stop by a public park with nice shade trees or somewhere with an attractive view and eat your lunch in your vehicle or on a picnic bench. While there, you might take a moment to compute your savings on meals over a month's time.

> **You are never too old to set another goal or to dream a new dream.**
>
> ***– C. S. Lewis***

42.

Get Out of the House!

After I was discharged from the military service, I worked at a number of assorted jobs before I found my calling. One of those jobs was selling insurance.

Every Friday morning there was a sales meeting at the insurance company's office.

One day, following the weekly meeting, I got caught up in a personal conversation with one of the agents and hadn't noticed that the other agents had already departed the building.

At that moment, the general manager approached, smiled and addressed the other agent and me.

"Gentleman," he began. "I've been with the company for 22 years, and up to this time, I've never seen a policy sold in this office. Now, please get out there and begin knocking on those doors!"

I daresay the same advice can be applied today to any business-minded individuals who take refuge inside the four walls of their home or apartment.

You'll be amazed at how much can be accomplished simply by being outside your home or office and exposed to real, live people.

More than once I've seen individuals take less-than-desirable temporary or part-time jobs simply to get out of the house and be in a place where they can meet and talk with an assortment of people.

One man I know in his forties and unemployed took a job busing tables in a restaurant. He earned a few dollars and made the acquaintance of other people.

Within a short time, he ingratiated himself with many of the regular diners by observing their special needs and tastes and providing exceptional service. He greeted customers by name, sometimes to the consternation of the servers who ranked above him, and he catered to these same diners within the bounds of his ability and duties. Needless to say, it didn't take him long to establish valuable contacts which resulted in his being boosted from the restaurant job to a more lucrative position where he remains today.

It turns out that this sort of good fortune also happened to me. Not long after I left the newspaper and was struggling to keep afloat, a woman who owned a mortgage investment company contacted me. She had remembered that a year earlier, when I was still at the newspaper, I had written a story about her business club that impressed her. She inquired about me through a third party and was informed that I was now freelancing. She subsequently contacted me and asked if I could produce a quarterly newsletter she could mail to her investors.

It wasn't something I had done before, but I was hungry and figured I could easily do this. Why not?

I wasted not a moment getting to her office for a scheduled meeting, then immediately began work on the first issue. Yes, you guessed it. The work was done on my kitchen table.

She proudly displayed the first issue to her fellow women's business club members and a few weeks later, I began receiving calls from some of them asking if I could meet to discuss a newsletter for their businesses.

Within a couple months time, I was producing employee and marketing newsletters for twenty Silicon Valley companies and needed to subcontract a good amount of the work.

Before that first phone call from the woman at the mortgage investment firm, I had no more thoughts about producing newsletters than making widgets. I was involved in book publishing and not showing much income from it. For the next 15 years, modest as it was, the newsletter production business provided me with a livable income.

Obviously, the moral of these stories is get out there and make all the contacts you can.

> **I know not age, nor weariness, nor defeat**
>
> ***– Rose Kennedy***

43.

For Those Who Help You

Although I have serious reservations about bestowing gifts or favors on my business customers or their representatives, I have just the opposite approach when it comes to expressing appreciation to vendors, subcontractors or anyone who helps me expand my business.

First, a brief word of explanation about providing gifts to customers. No matter what your intentions might be, there is always the issue of appearance. Maybe the gift or favor might not be seen as a bribe or incentive by you or the recipient, but it could easily be seen as inappropriate or a conflict of interest by the recipient's boss or co-workers. For that reason alone, my advice is *don't do it.* Notes or letters of thanks are okay. But, when you cross that line and get into tangible gifts, you're looking for problems.

However, it's just the opposite when it comes to your vendors and subcontractors.

These are the people you've decided to hang onto because they're honest, reliable, fair and treat you like a fellow human being, not a number. Others that have come your way are only memories because they didn't meet these standards.

Once, when I told my Uncle Max about how a vendor, in this instance a repairman, saved me from incurring a huge expense, he replied, "George, you cannot be *too nice* to this man."

So, I go the extra step to show my gratitude. I send thank you cards whenever a job is especially well done or a vendor meets a tight deadline for me.

At the very least, I always find time to express my appreciation when a vendor does something extraordinary to warrant a compliment.

Sometimes, I'll present him or her with a gift certificate for a dinner for two at their favorite restaurant. I do this only occasionally and when it seems suitable.

As mentioned in Chapter 135 and in other content in this book, I always attempt to pay vendors and subcontractors by return mail (big companies and government can wait until the due date). This is yet another way of expressing my gratitude.

> **Consult not your fears but your hopes and your dreams. Think not about your frustrations, but about your unfulfilled potential. Concern yourself not with what you tried and failed in, but with what it is still possible for you to do.**
>
> ***– Pope John XXIII***

44.

The Door County Model

This is a term that I coined after having seen it work firsthand for those who live and work in Door County, a resort community in Wisconsin, where the summer tourist business drives almost the entire economy.

For many years, my wife spent her summer vacations on this delightful Wisconsin peninsula that sticks out like a long finger surrounded by 350 miles of Lake Michigan and Green Bay shoreline.

From June through September, thousands of vacationers, mostly from the metropolitan Chicago and Milwaukee areas, escape the summer heat by getting away to Door County and its cooler temperatures.

Streets are crowded and room vacancies are few. However, in winter there are times when you can roll a bowling ball down the street of one of the many Door County villages.

But year-round, the residents still need to pay their rent and buy shoes for the kids.

For the 27,000 permanent residents of Door County it's a cyclical pattern of "feast or famine."

During the three months of peak season, there's always a shortage of hospitality workers. So the permanent residents can pick and choose the jobs they like and that offer the best compensation.

But, it's a different story during the remaining eight or nine months of the year when tourism amounts to only a fraction of what it is during the peak months.

It's only then that the Door County Model can be fully seen. Since only some tourist facilities are open, and usually only on the weekends, the few permanent residents, many who have families to support, manage to cobble together a living by working at several part-time jobs such as driving the school bus, operating snow plows, performing handyman repairs and maintenance for absentee owners of summer cabins and cottages along with an assortment of other part-time jobs.

They also make jams and hand crafts to sell in the shops the next season and give guitar lessons, etc.

Many also derive steady off-season income by contracting with absentee owners to make weekly checks of their vacation homes. This service is a "must" for owners because during a hard freeze their water pipes can burst, resulting in major damage.

Combining long work hours during the summer with whatever part-time work they can find in the off-season, these folks manage to carve out a modest income and at the same time enjoy living and raising their families in an unspoiled and healthy environment.

So, how does this affect you since you're probably not intending to move to Door County or to a similar tourist destination?

The answer is that no matter what the condition of your economic circumstances, you can begin today to launch the Door County Model as your personal game plan while continuing to send out resumes and seek employment in your own area of specialty. And… and here's the bonus *and…* you can at the same time start building your own business.

Yes, you can do all of these at once. You just need to strategically manage your time and stay focused.

And when you're not working as an employee at a part-time job, you need to be giving maximum attention to your own small business startup which can replace the part-time jobs in the future.

Meanwhile, if you find a good-paying, full-time job in your field and decide that's the best way for you to go, you haven't lost anything.

45.

Play the Percentages

Anyone who has at one time or another taken an interest in the finer points of baseball strategy knows that a successful manager almost always adheres to what is commonly called *playing the percentages.*

If you have a runner on first base and your team is behind, you almost automatically instruct your batter to sacrifice bunt in order to advance the runner to scoring position. Baseball managers who don't respect the percentages usually don't last long in their jobs, assuming that they could even qualify for such a job in the first place.

Playing the percentages also applies big time in your survival strategy. Here's why:

Suppose you've been laid off at age 52 and you're hoping to get another job in your field that pays as well as the job you lost. To begin with, the percentages tell you that only a small number of those laid off in this age group have a possibility of reestablishing themselves in their field. That doesn't mean that you have *no* chance. But the possibilities are slim.

Should that discourage you from sending out resumes and searching some of the appropriate online websites for potential openings? Absolutely not. Carry on. But at the same time set in motion a strategy that enables you to play the percentages to your advantage.

What this means is that you meanwhile try to line up all of the part-time or temporary employment that you can manage by invoking The Door County Model cited in the previous chapter as you simultaneously grow your fledgling business. Honest. It's not that hard. You arrange your opportunities in order of priority. First come jobs that bring money into the house. These jobs receive top priority whether they're part-time for four hours a week and pay minimum wage or work coming from your new business. And if you receive a call from a prospective customer who appears ready to do business, I categorize such a call *top priority* and scramble to get the work before he or she has a change of mind.

Applying for part-time jobs and soliciting customers for your own business are next on the priority ladder.

And finally, when you're not out working for pay or applying for jobs or soliciting customers for your own business, then you might use your time to take advantage of some of the money-saving opportunities which you'll find in Part III of this book.

However, we haven't forgotten about playing the percentages.

The occasions when you'll need the quick instincts of a successful team manager come when you face an either-or situation. You might be working on two or three different part-time or temporary jobs and have started a small business. Suddenly, you receive a phone call from a headhunter who has a listing for a job in your field. Unfortunately, not only is the job five states away, but the pay is about 60 percent of what you were earning at the job you lost. How do you respond?

This is where probability percentages — just like those that baseball managers rely on for their decisions — come into play.

First question: Will the company pay to move you and your family? Will they give you a contract for a specific number of years?

When you've weighed the benefits and the risks of taking the position, ask yourself if it warrants making the move and giving up your small business along with the piecemeal jobs that you've cobbled together?

What is the percentage of probability or likelihood that Choice A (accepting the headhunter's offer) will be turn out to be a better option than Choice B (sticking with your current situation)?

This would be an appropriate time to consult all the wise men and women you know, listen carefully to their sage counsel and then make the final decision together with your spouse.

In almost thirty years of marriage, my wife and I have never had cause to regret a decision we've reached in this manner.

> **I'd rather attempt to do something great and fail than to attempt to do nothing and succeed.**
>
> ***– Robert H. Schuller***

46.

Find a Need and Fill It

As you find yourself in the process of thinking about starting a small business, one where you don't require startup capital and can operate from home, you might consider this old slogan, "Find a need and fill it."

In Chapter 16, you'll recall that I recommended that you acquire copies of Jay Conrad Levinson's various self-help books, including *555 Ways to Earn Extra Money.*

Many, if not most, of Levinson's *555 Ways* don't require either startup capital or a commercial location. Most are home-based businesses.

When you're sorting through your options, keep foremost in mind that you don't want to get involved in anything that competes with big box stores such as Walmart, Costco or other large chains. If any chain offers what you have in mind for your new business, move on to the next idea.

When I moved from the East Coast to the San Francisco Bay Area in the 1970s, I was young, unattached and seeking activities for singles. This pursuit required time and some effort, but ultimately I found my ideal affinity groups — hiking clubs.

Then one weekend, while on a Sierra Club trek, a hiker I knew complained to me about being unable to find other activities for singles and asked me if I knew of any such groups. He asked the right person. I had kept notes during my search the previous few months and I offered to send him photocopies of my notes.

Later, I thought, "Hey, my gathered information might be a valuable resource!" I pondered my next move. Then, I went into action.

I began running a standing classified ad in the personals column of the combined Sunday *San Francisco Examiner* and *Chronicle* in which I offered a printed listing of singles activities for a very modest price.

Every week, I'd find between 25 and 40 checks in my mailbox from Bay Area singles.

After five years of modest though steady profit, the owner of a computer dating company made an offer to buy my little business — an offer I couldn't refuse.

That was the first of a number of part-time, home-based businesses that I launched. In the interest of disclosure, not all were successful, but a number of them were.

The upshot here is that there are always opportunities for niche businesses where there's almost no competition.

Keep your eyes open for these little gems.

I know a handyman; I'll call him Bill, who also does landscape maintenance and painting. If one of his customers asks for a recommendation of someone to build them a birdhouse or enclose a carport, etc., he'll respond with, "Yes, I can do that." I've seldom seen him turn down any job. And, yes, he's good. My wife jokes that she'll let Bill do anything except take out her appendix.

And by the way, Bill is occupied all the time. His prices are reasonable and he's accommodating — a perfect combination for success.

As you read further in this book, you'll come across numerous examples of other successful niche businesses.

These examples show that even in this upside down economy, if you can develop and keep that same can-do attitude that Bill holds, you can be self-employed and earn a decent living.

47.

Expect Failures

No sooner have I told you about successes than I now caution you about business failures. You need to know that failure is part of the price of doing business and you should be prepared for it.

No one bats 1.000; and that includes you.

But that doesn't mean that when a venture isn't successful that you must incur a big loss. The trick is knowing how to test an idea without committing either a lot of money or time.

Merchandisers who rely on direct mail will often have access to a mailing list, for example, of 20,000 beekeepers or 50,000 veterinary clinics. They'll prepare a complete direct mail list, but initially mail to only 2,000 names on the list. The computer-selected names are spread across the country to provide a cross-section. If the test mailing produces a certain percentage of orders, usually at least a two percent return, then the merchandiser will likely mail to 5,000 or 10,000 more prospects on one of the lists. If the returns continue to remain good, he'll ultimately mail to the entire list. This way, in the event of failure, his loss is limited to the expense of the initial test mailing.

You can follow a similar pattern, assuring that any losses are minimal.

When I was a newspaper reporter, I once interviewed one of the most successful businessmen on the San Francisco Peninsula. His name was John Rickey, and I talked with him on the occasion of his ninetieth birthday.

Reflecting on his rich and colorful life, he told me how he was sent to America alone as a ten-year-old in the steerage compartment of a trans-Atlantic vessel. After his arrival, he slept in the storage room of a delicatessen in New Jersey where he worked as a child laborer.

He also recounted a bankruptcy he experienced after he'd established himself in business, adding "I believe that everyone needs to go broke at least once to truly understand what business is all about."

Although there might be a lot of truth to this, I would point to the other side of the coin. You need to be right only once, and it can be your ticket to future stability and sustainability.

Don't let the fear of failure hamper you.

> **The key is to keep company only with people who uplift you, whose presence calls forth your best.**
>
> ***– Epictetus***

48.

Learn from the Experience of Others

You need only switch on the TV news to see a report on a local or national crisis and ask yourself, "Didn't they learn a lesson after this same thing happened a few years ago?" No, sometimes people don't learn. But you can and must.

Throughout life I have come to observe that when it comes to learning there are three types of individuals.

There are those who are able to learn from the experiences of others, those who can learn only from their own experiences and those who neither learn from the experience of others nor from their own experiences.

Those in the first category are my role models. I admire those who, when confronted with a question or issue, are quick to turn to an Internet search engine and glean everything they can on a particular subject. Or they might contact an expert who has been there before, so to speak, and can share their knowledge gained from real-life experience.

However, it has always seemed to me that the bulk of society prefers to "do-it-yourself" rather than seek advice, even advice from an expert or other authoritative source.

Finally, there are those in the last category who are unable to learn through any of the aforementioned approaches and continue to repeat the same mistakes ad infinitum. Thankfully, they account for only a small percentage of the total population. Many of these individuals are challenged by a myriad of deep-set problems which sometimes can be helped only by a professional.

If you're in the first group, carry on. You're on the right track, and you won't be wasting your time, energy or money on endeavors where others have already reported failure.

If you're in that second group — those who can learn only from their own experiences — you might take a moment the next time your instincts thrust you into action, and consider first gathering some information and expert data as to whether your idea has already been tried and if so, what were the results?

> **Those who fail to learn from the lessons of history are condemned to repeat its failures.**
>
> ***– George Santayana***

49.

Protecting Your Receivables

Never let any customer owe you more money than you can afford to lose. Make no exceptions as just one mistake can wipe you out and leave you worse off financially than you could ever imagine.

These words of advice were given to me by a relative who had weathered 40 years in business and had remained solvent throughout.

I took his advice to heart, and over the fifteen years that I operated The Newsletter Group in Silicon Valley, I billed more than $1 million and never lost a single penny due to a customer's failure to pay.

While I realize that in today's economy that's not an impressive figure, even for a home-based business, I wonder how many businesses large or small can boast such a record.

As noted in an earlier chapter, I insisted on "progress payments" from my customers. I quickly found that any business-person or manager with honest intentions doesn't balk at such a request. The requirement is logical, practical and fair. If they won't agree to your terms, back off immediately.

These were my payment terms: If a company wanted me to produce an employee or marketing newsletter, I'd require payment for one-third of the total amount upon approval of draft copy; another third on approval of press proofs and the balance within 30 days of delivery of the newsletter.

If the scheduled payments weren't forthcoming as agreed, I wouldn't proceed.

Over the 15-year span, two companies filed for bankruptcy. But, because both companies had already paid for two-thirds of their newsletters in production, their bankruptcy trustee managed somewhere to dig up the funds needed to complete the issues. My company was paid in full while other vendors were scrambling for a place in line to collect what might have ended up as pennies on the dollar.

I had a friend who had a larger and more established business than mine, but fell victim to his largest account, a company that accounted for more than 70 percent of his total receivables. When it filed for bankruptcy, he received nothing and suffered financially for several years thereafter.

This is precisely why, *Don't let anyone owe you more than you can afford to lose*, remains the best advice you'll ever receive on this subject.

Especially beware if you find yourself in this situation: One of your biggest customer's account is overdue, but they still want more of your merchandise or services. You're afraid that if you cut them off they'll never pay your bill and you might need to go to court, which is often to no avail anyway. So hoping that they'll pay you soon, you continue to provide them with merchandise or services. Finally, you find that you've been stuck for even more worthless receivables when the company declares bankruptcy.

Set your stop-loss parameters and stick to them. Explain to your customer that you're a "small fish" and have inadequate resources to bankroll them. You can also explain that by not having to bankroll your customers, you can avoid financial risks and losses, thereby enabling you to provide them with merchandise or services at a rate well below what they might pay someone else.

If this relates to an existing customer whose account is overdue, explain that you'll be pleased to resume doing business with them when they've brought their account up to date.

If they don't pay, take your loss, which will likely be a modest loss because you've heeded the above advice and protected yourself by requiring progress payments.

50.

Be Your Own Warren Buffet

Although my fledgling business might have been minuscule when compared to the corporate giants, I nevertheless often found myself thinking in terms that might befit a Warren Buffet or the founder of Starbucks, Howard Schultz.

I would sometimes ask myself how would these notables have reacted in a situation I found myself facing at the moment?

Should I expand here or there or explore a new territory or product? I'd wonder what would Buffet or Schultz do in such a situation.

I must confess that I enjoyed every moment that I worked for myself and continue to do so. The same goes for one of my closest friends.

We sometimes remind ourselves how stifled we felt when we were employed in the corporate world and under someone else's thumb.

Exercise your freedom and enjoy it. It's one of the many benefits of being your own boss.

> **I never attempt to make money on the stock market. I buy on the assumption that they could close the market the next day and not reopen it for ten years.**
>
> ***– Warren Buffett***

51.

The New Normal

Just a few weeks ago, a friend was flying between Chicago and Los Angeles and found himself seated next to two men who appeared to be corporate executives.

He overheard one say to the other, "Yes, I have an assistant, too. She's really good. We work her pretty hard. Sometimes 80 hours a week. But we pay her well."

This is yet another example of what is being called "The New Normal."

If you or a member of your family is looking for a good-paying job, it's likely you'll find that today's "normal" is that the company is seeking a young work force, perfectly composed of single individuals with no children or family responsibilities. They'll be expected to work long hours and "voluntarily" work at least half days on Saturday. Nine-to-five types need not apply.

If you're working for low wages in fast food or at a discount big-box store or if you're driving a delivery truck, the above description probably doesn't fit. But do you want to work for just above minimum wage?

And what are your chances of finding security or stability in such jobs?

In February 2014, *The New York Times* cited a study reporting that approximately 20 percent of all new businesses were started by entrepreneurs aged 50 to 59 years, and 15 percent were 60 and over. The *Times* article concluded that conditions in the current job market are so difficult for those over 50 that more workers in this age group are now forced to pursue entrepreneurial endeavors.

52.

Your Own Online Business

There's money to be made — with virtually no capital required — in launching a store or catalog online. Repeat: *only* online.

No merchandise or stock to buy or maintain. No printed catalogs to go out in the mail. No initial investment other than your time and hiring a person to design your website — or perhaps you can do the website yourself.

Suppose you learn that folks engaged in a particular hobby must shop around for their supplies. And suppose that you learn from talking with these hobbyists exactly what supplies they require.

Then, you contact the various wholesale suppliers, distributors or manufacturers and line up a system for arranging what are known as "drop shipments."

You prepare a catalog that appears only online and you promote it among the hobbyists.

They order their supplies from you and you forward the order to your source along with payment.

Then, your source ships directly to the hobbyist using your label which you provide. Of course, you price the item so that there's a profit built in for you.

You need keep no stock on hand. Remember, the term is *drop ship.*

While not every wholesaler or manufacturer will agree to this arrangement, many will. You'll need to find them.

To eliminate the website and web design cost, you might first want to check out eBay. In addition to enabling sellers to list their items without charge (a commission is collected if the item sells), eBay also provides more active sellers with online "stores" where they can list multiple items. There may or may not be a setup fee in addition to the normal commission applied to all sales.

However, the setup is so simple that it doesn't require the services of a web designer. And it will save you costs.

I recently talked to an eBay online store owner who specializes in electric shavers and replacement parts. As luck would have it, he had in stock a replacement rotary blade set for a Norelco shaver which I have and is at least 40 years old and still running well.

I expressed amazement that he had such a replacement available as I had searched everywhere and couldn't locate one. He responded that he had spotted a carton containing about 50 of these sets among items in a dispersal sale.

"If I had a hundred of these, I could easily sell them," said the owner. "Right now, I'm down to my last few."

There are also specialty websites and online stores for such items as suspenders, shoe laces and nightcaps.

Take for example AbeBooks.com, which likely maintains the world's largest database of used books. Thousands of independent and home-based booksellers list books in its database. When you find the book you're searching for, you place your order through AbeBooks. They collect payment and then send the order, less commission, to the independent bookseller who mails the book to you. Yet another example of drop shipping.

The best example of such a niche business that I can recall is this one. When the clock on our old GE range quit and couldn't be repaired, our handyman contacted GE's parts department, but was informed that parts for that 24-year-old model were no longer stocked.

Our handyman learned further that when repair parts have been on the shelf a certain number of years (perhaps 20 years or more), they are normally removed and sold in bulk to the highest bidder.

Our handyman was in luck that day and was given the name of the successful bidder for the old GE oven parts. It turned out to be a man who lived in the country and raised chickens for a living.

When our handyman phoned him, the man wrote down the part number, then explained that he had to go out to his barn and try to find the part.

An hour later, he phoned back saying that he had a brand new GE clock, still in the original box, and could ship it the next day. His price was reasonable, and the clock is still working.

These specialty and niche businesses abound. You, too, can dip your toe in the water with little risk. If you hit it right, you can enjoy extra income for years while continuing to build up your other ventures.

> **You create your opportunities by asking for them.**
>
> ***– Shakti Gawain***

53.

The Advantages of Timing

You've heard the saying that timing is everything. Well, often it can indeed be your friend if you know how to use it to your advantage.

Suppose you're looking for a sub-contractor or supplier to provide goods or services for a project which you're quoting.

The amount of your quote may often depend on the quote or bid you are given by a sub-contractor or supplier you've approached.

If the sub-contractor is busy, he may quote you a higher price than he would if business were slow. This is why it pays to shop around.

On several occasions, when their businesses entered a slow period, contractors have acknowledged to me that they underbid their competitors by several hundred dollars because they had a couple of good workers who weren't occupied and they wanted to keep them busy. They'd rather make little or nothing on such a job, the aim being to provide steady employment for their workers. The last thing they want to do is to send one of their good workers home. Then, when business returns to normal, the boss won't have to recruit new employees.

Timing is important and can make a difference in how much you pay for goods or services.

54.

Take Care of Your Customers

Taking care of your customers means going beyond showing up and doing the job competently. It's also about letting them know that you care.

Listen to their problems and concerns. Very possibly there's no one else who will, and that might also include their own family members.

If this surprises you, you aren't alone.

It seems that at least once a week I encounter an individual somewhere who wants to tell me their life story, including their frustrations and disappointments. They obviously need to vent. They need empathy and understanding.

Perhaps, the most memorable such experience that occurred wasn't in the office of one of my customers, but at a wedding reception.

My wife and I had just finished eating our buffet dinner, the professional DJ's music had begun and people were dancing and moving about.

An older man, obviously of retirement age, soon approached our table. We gave him a welcoming smile, and in response he wasted no time in asking if one of the chairs opposite us was occupied. We informed him that it wasn't and beckoned him to take a seat.

What followed was an exceptionally poignant experience for me and my wife.

The man described his six-year-old granddaughter and told us that she was the apple of his eye.

At the same time, he removed from his coat pocket a worn envelope containing photos of his granddaughter and even more photos of playground equipment, including an elaborate playhouse, that he'd custom-built in his home workshop.

Throughout the conversation, he never mentioned his wife or his adult children. It was obvious that this man felt very alone and that no one paid him any attention. He seemed almost desperate to find someone who would listen to him and offer a kind word.

We both did our best to boost his spirits by oohing and ahhing each time he displayed a different photo of his woodworking creations.

After almost an hour, a woman in his party approached and informed him that they were leaving. However, before departing, he took a long moment to deliver a heartfelt "thank you" for taking time to look at his photos.

To this day we still discuss this experience and cite it as the example of one of those shortcomings in our society that needs fixing.

So, what's this got to do with operating a successful business?

If you're out among the public and calling on customers and prospects, you'll most certainly encounter folks who need to talk to someone who will patiently listen.

And if you're up to active listening — not everyone is — you can accomplish two things. First, it will make you an altruist. You'll be making a positive contribution to the life of someone in need. And you know the saying that "what goes around comes around."

Secondly, your kindness could result in your turning a customer into a friend. Who better to recommend you to others?

Buy a copy of Dale Carnegie's *How to Win Friends and Influence People.*

Don't be put off by the fact that the book has been around for more than eighty years. The book's contents are as valid today as they were then.

If you follow the book's advice, your customers will value you beyond just your usefulness as a vendor. People today are not looking for just another stone face or robot-like character. There are more than enough of such people to go around.

Many hunger for an empathetic soul to listen to them, if only for a few minutes.

By being a good and empathetic listener, you can help others and at the same time help yourself.

There's a second important aspect to taking care of your customers. Needless to say, you always want to do the very best job you can do. But, you can go beyond that. When a customer phones you late on Friday afternoon and informs you that he desperately needs a repair or a certain piece of merchandise, and everyone has already closed for the weekend, you can be a hero by responding, "Sam, I was just about to head out for the lake. But, I can't leave you here facing this situation without help. I'll be over in a few minutes, and I can leave for the lake tomorrow."

Where do you think that will place your standing with Sam and his company?

> **Fortune may have yet a better success in reserve for you, and they who lose today may win tomorrow.**
>
> ***– Miguel de Cervantes***

55.

Some Businesses to Avoid

When you establish your business, make sure it's home-based, that you don't have to pay rent and that you can call on your customers rather than having them call on you.

You don't want a retail establishment where you have no control over who walks in and out of your door.

Nor do you want to pay the monthly rent on a retail site or sign a lease you'll be stuck with if things don't work out.

Whatever you decide to do, stay out of the restaurant and/or fast food business. Both are filled with headaches and represent a ticket to personal burnout and an almost assured financial loss. Not to mention the long hours together with few, if any, days off.

Over the years, restaurants have consistently been shown to have the highest mortality rate of all new businesses.

Best choices: Either sell a product that you can ship to your customers from your home or provide a service where you go to your customer.

56.

Who Can You Trust?

I once worked for a boss whose instructions to me before I departed on an assignment were brief: "Trust no one. Take names. And get it in writing."

When I heard that, I thought his instructions were perhaps extreme, but over the next 20 to 30 years most of them began to make good sense.

In these litigious times, you can't be too careful. You must always be thinking about liability and the possibility of getting sued for negligence.

And, what about taking names and getting it in writing?

One of the most satisfying experiences I can recall came when I was waiting in line for a rental car at Los Angeles International Airport.

I carried in my pocket a detailed itinerary, so when I checked the rental contract handed to me for signature and saw that the daily rental price was substantially higher than the rate that was confirmed via phone, I challenged it. This was before email, so I had no email confirmation on paper that I could hand over as proof of the original agreement.

When I questioned the rate and quoted my earlier conversation with the toll-free 800 number reservationist who confirmed the rate, I was asked by the counter representative, "Well, who did you speak with?"

How many people remember who they spoke with several weeks ago?

As it turned out, I'd followed my old boss' instructions from years back and I had all that information on my prepared itinerary.

I promptly cited the reservationist's first and last name and the time and date of the conversation.

The counter agent, obviously taken by surprise, retreated to a back office, held a conversation with a supervisor, then returned and changed the rental price back to the original figure.

So, in the end, my old boss had it right after all.

> **Persist — don't take no for an answer. If you're happy to sit at your desk and not take any risk, you'll be sitting at your desk for the next 20 years**
>
> ***– David Rubenstein***

57.

Sweeten the Deal

If you've quoted a price for a job or for something you might be selling and your prospective customer appears to be on the fence as to whether to go ahead, consider offering him or her a free trial of your product or service.

To be clear, I'm not suggesting that you take this step every time you make a presentation or submit a quote for a job, but *only* when you sense that the prospective customer is on the fence. Give them a reason to jump to your side.

Perhaps, he or she is afraid that if they give you the green light that they might later regret the decision and risk criticism from higher up.

You can eliminate prospects' concerns by assuring them that if they're not fully satisfied after the trial period, they're under no obligation to continue or reorder.

I rarely extended such a freebie, but when I did I usually got the business.

A word of caution: *You* must be the one to make the free trial offer. If the prospective customer requests it, nix it immediately. It's a sign that this person wants to get something for nothing, and no good will come of it.

58.

When This Happens, Don't Waste Your Time

If you're in the business of performing a service, expect to receive requests for bids.

However, you might be surprised to discover that in many instances these requests amount to no more than an unpaid extra drain on your time as well as a waste of your money.

That's because most of these requests for bids will come from either a corporation or a government agency. And in each case there will exist in that office a standing rule or policy that for expenditures above a certain minimum amount, three bids must be obtained.

And you'll find that in most instances the corporation or government agency has a contractor with whom they've been doing business for years and to whom they want to give the work. However, part of the game is that the office must follow the rules by obtaining three bids. And again, surprise, but in most instances the office requesting the bids is *not* required to accept the lowest bid. They're permitted to apply other criteria in making their choice.

So, bottom line is that this usually leaves you out.

How do I handle these bid requests? I usually respond to the person on the phone by saying that right now I'm very busy and don't have time to submit a formal bid. However, for whatever it's worth, this is what my charges or fee would be. Thanks for calling.

Then there's another ploy used by bid seekers which is even more devious. You receive a call, usually from someone employed in the private sector, asking if you can perform a certain service for them. They don't even ask you about price, but instead move right into inquiring if you could appear before this or that committee and make a presentation detailing your proposal. And, of course, bring all your good ideas along.

Some of these individuals might be under the impression that I was born yesterday, but I keep my emotions in line and reply in a courteous manner: "I'd like to be able to do that. But, I'm a one-man company and I have to make every hour of my time count. My normal fee is $75.00 an hour. If you want me to prepare such a proposal, I'd be pleased to do it at my hourly rate plus materials. After I deliver the presentation, your company is under no obligation to hire me for further services and everything that I bring to the presentation, including my ideas, are yours to keep."

I can report that in over fifteen years not one of these conversations continued beyond the moment I delivered this response.

Also, I can attest that to this day I've never received one piece of business from any of the individuals who phoned me requesting bids, let alone a call back for additional information.

Be alert for exploiters!

> **There is no passion to be found playing small — in settling for a life that is less than the one you are capable of living.**
>
> ***– Nelson Mandela***

59.

Honest Work Isn't Beneath You

Remember the Door County model? Another source of added income that can put some money in your pocket is pet sitting or house sitting.

We have a dog and we've engaged dog sitters and house sitters on numerous occasions. With daytime residential break-ins on the increase, we'd never leave our house unoccupied. And we'd never place our dog in a kennel or so-called doggie resort.

Fees for pet sitting in either your home or the dog owner's home vary depending on where you reside.

There are numerous ways to advertise your services — all for free — using Internet resources such as craigslist.org and social media and by posting 3x5 cards in appropriate locations.

Also, let veterinarian offices and pet grooming services know you're available for pet sitting and be sure to stop in and thank them for any referrals.

Again, this is another one of those opportunities you can't afford to view as being beneath you or allow yourself to be concerned about what your friends might say or think. Remind yourself that they aren't responsible for paying your bills.

60.

Incorporate or LLC?

As with other business decisions, there are advantages and disadvantages to incorporating.

Advantages include protection from personal liability, tax breaks and yet another that few independent entrepreneurs consider. That being that large businesses and corporations often prefer to outsource their work to small businesses that are already incorporated or established as an LLC (limited liability company).

Why? Because in recent years the IRS has cracked down on the practice of businesses hiring people under the classification of "independent contractor" when in fact these people do the same work as permanent employees, except at lower pay and without benefits.

The IRS offers a definition of what constitutes an independent contractor, and if they find that a business has been fudging on this issue they can require the business to pay some hefty penalties.

However, when a large business or corporation engages a small or independent business — be it only a single individual — to handle some of its outsource work, the requirements for sending the individual a 1099 form at the end of the year are more liberal and relaxed if that person's business is incorporated as a subchapter-S corporation or registered as an LLC. Often, if a large business intends to outsource some of its work, it might prefer to engage an individual who has a company or corporate name rather than raise a red flag by handing the work to Tom Jones or Mary Smith, which then begs the thorny question of whether Tom Jones or Mary Smith is considered an "independent contractor" under the IRS definition or should be considered a company employee.

Knowing this can work in your favor if you are seeking outsource work from a large company.

For purposes of background, you should know that in some tax years, the IRS has required that 1099s be sent to virtually everyone the business paid, in any amount, and in other years the rules haven't required that.

You should also know that being incorporated as a subchapter-S or registered as an LLC doesn't necessarily mean that you as an individual pay lower taxes.

But there are options that enable individuals and small businesses to lower their state income taxes, especially if the business is located in a state that has high taxes. For example, an entrepreneur who lived and operated in a state with one of the highest state income tax rates set up two corporations. In his own high tax state, he created a company I'll call Red, Inc. This was the company that performed the work and brought in the money.

But, then Red, Inc. contracted with a Nevada corporation, his second LLC named Black, Inc., for various services. Nevada is among the lowest tax states. A large part of Red, Inc.'s income was paid to Black, Inc. although the actual work might have been performed anywhere, including in the entrepreneur's home state. Billings came from the Nevada entity and payments were sent and banked there. The entrepreneur avoided paying a substantial amount of state income tax, but his federal income tax liability remained unchanged.

You can also find tax saving strategies by placing income property in the name of an LLC and renting space from the LLC for your business. The tax savings comes in because rental income enjoys a depreciation allowance provided in the tax code and at the moment is also exempt from paying Social Security tax. Of course, the amount of rent you pay must be reasonable and in line with similar rents in the area.

One of the disadvantages of incorporation is that you must maintain a separate bank account and file a separate tax return for the entity.

Most small businesses today register as an LLC. It is the least costly way and often you can fill out the papers yourself. Recently, the Arizona Corporation Commission announced that applicants for LLC status could fill out and submit their applications online. In many states, kits for this purpose are available online at a nominal charge.

Of course, there remains the option to incorporate as a subchapter-S corporation (available to small business) or as a C-corporation which is usually the option for larger companies and organizations. Talk about this with your accountant.

WARNING: If you plan to operate in the State of California, beware. California has the highest registration fee and ongoing annual fee for corporations large or small. If you incorporate in California, you can expect to pay an initial fee close to $1,000 and pay the same amount each year for renewal. And if you decide to incorporate in a less expensive state and still do business in California, you'll be required to register and pay virtually the same fee because you are considered a foreign company doing business in California. If you're a Californian, consider all your options and talk to some savvy advisers before you make a move.

61.

What's the Greatest Word?

Years ago, a wise businessman revealed to me a secret. He informed me that the greatest word in the English language is *free.* He was probably right. But, I have come up with my own nomination for the runner-up award. That word is *affordable.*

If you intend to make a success of your business, especially if you'll be performing a service, consider adding the word *Affordable* in front of whatever name you've planned. Such as Affordable Landscape Design, Affordable Plumbing or Heating or Cooling, Affordable Cabinetry or Affordable Pet Sitting.

And if someone in your community has already staked out that name, then consider Smith Affordable Landscape Design or Smith Affordable Plumbing.

In these hard economic times, many individuals are forced to watch their expenses more carefully and shop around for a price they can afford.

You're operating a home-based business and don't have the overhead of an established business, but you can still manage a fair profit while making your services available to the cost-conscious.

62.

If Lightning Strikes a Second Time

Every day, I see on TV or read in the newspaper about how those laid off are being encouraged to train for a new career.

If you're 25 or 32 or 34 and reading this, then perhaps training for a new career might be the right move for you.

However, if you're over 40, the idea of a major career change should give you pause for thought, and with good reason.

Where do you find companies recruiting new employees in their late forties, fifties and sixties? I know that hamburger and fast-food chain executives like to be quoted as saying that mature individuals make good workers. They're reliable and they show up in time for work, etc.

Wonderful! But, how are you going to get by with a minimum wage job and for how long can you perform that kind of work?

Forgive me for my skepticism, but it's my opinion that these claims about new careers for all is smoke and mirrors — mostly illusions — with little basis in fact.

Recently, a government inquiry into private sector educational programs that train individuals for new careers found that many students spent two years in programs for which there were no jobs when they graduated. Worse yet, students ended up owing thousands of dollars for training that many couldn't hope to repay.

Which brings me to the all-important question: Suppose you enroll in a training program for a new career. And suppose you devote several months time and possibly part with some of your savings to complete the program. Meanwhile you're not bringing in income. And if you surmount all these obstacles and land a job, what happens if lightning (misfortune) strikes again in the form of layoffs and you again find yourself unemployed? How many blows of this type can you afford to take in your lifetime and still be able to pick yourself up off the floor?

My answer to this question, which you can guess, is that if it were me, training for a new career would represent an unacceptable risk and that I'd be far better off establishing my own independent business with much greater probabilities for survival.

> **Be thine own palace, or the world's thy jail.**
>
> ***– John Donne***

63.

Avoid These Jobs!

Although taking any honest job that doesn't put you on the other side of the law is preferable to sitting at home, there are exceptions. There are jobs — both full time and part time — that I consider too dangerous to consider.

What are they? Two examples are driving a cab or working in a convenience market, especially on the night shift.

Under no circumstances would I recommend considering either of these jobs. You need only read about the daily beatings, robberies and murders of individuals in these high-risk jobs to make you realize that these are not for you.

Better to flip hamburgers or work in another fast food environment for minimum wage until you can find a better job or get your own business rolling.

Personal safety is paramount. Remember this for your own sake and your family's, too.

> **I've always tried to go a step past wherever people expected me to end up.**
>
> ***– Beverly Sills***

64.

Brainstorming Pays Off

The smartest people I know don't come up with brilliant ideas or make intelligent decisions exclusively on their own. They brainstorm with friends, family members and others who are as smart and experienced as they are, even if they work in a different field.

Individuals who have egos that don't permit brainstorming with others are hobbling themselves, but often don't know it.

I received my first tips on how to brainstorm with others from a newspaper article written almost a half-century ago by Theodore Sorensen, an aide to President John F. Kennedy, who detailed for readers how the Kennedy Administration made decisions on critical issues.

According to Sorensen, JFK would summon his top advisers to the cabinet room and begin by posing this question: What are all the facts surrounding this issue?

The next question was: What is our goal here?

After further discussion around the long table and after the description of the goal had been sufficiently narrowed, the next question he posed was: What are the various options available for reaching this goal and what are the risks?

Discussion of this question alone could sometimes require a few hours.

Once all of the options and their risks were placed on the table, JFK and his advisors began discussing all of the possible outcomes associated with each option, both good and bad, and the possible costs and risks associated with those outcomes.

The final question was: Which of these options holds the best chance for success and preferably carries the lowest risk?

When the discussion was finished and everyone had had an opportunity to deliver an opinion, the meeting was adjourned.

But, usually a second session was called within a couple days, at which time the President would inform the same panel that he had arrived at a tentative decision.

After sharing this decision with the panel members, he'd go around the table and ask each member to tell him whether they were in agreement, and if they didn't agree, he urged them to tell him why.

According to Sorensen, JFK wasn't averse to changing his mind if someone pointed out to him a risk or other red flag that hadn't been considered earlier.

Over the years, any time I've had to make a critical decision, I've always followed the JFK model, although admittedly I didn't have either the number or caliber of advisers that were present in Kennedy's cabinet room.

In fact, though, I've added to the process as a result of a serendipitous experience. One day, when promoting a new book, I was trying to figure out what my chances of success were if I invested in several different bulk mailings simultaneously but using different mailing lists, each aimed at a different demographic.

As it turned out, I had the good fortune of discussing this idea with an extremely bright scientist/mathematician who held several PhDs, and just happened to be visiting my friend.

Without batting an eye, he took me through a formula based on my chances of failure with each of the separate mailings combined with a multiplier. He informed me that if I sent out all the test mailings that I'd described to him, a certain number of the test mailings would fail, but the chances of *all* the test mailings failing was less than five percent. Sure enough, his computations were correct. Three of the five mailings failed to produce sufficient response, one broke even and the last returned a very encouraging response rate. Of course, that's the demographic which we later pursued with gusto and found that subsequent mailings to that same list paid off handsomely for years to come and brought us significant repeat business.

As a consequence, my life experience has told me that you can never get too much feedback or listen to too many suggestions from thoughtful, informed sources that have your best interests at heart.

You must tell yourself that you can afford to listen to such advice and input because you know that in the end, the final decision will be yours.

> **I don't believe you have to be better than everybody else. I believe you have to be better than you ever thought you could be.**
>
> ***– Ken Venturi***

65.

Best Websites for Small Business

The Internet offers hundreds of websites and blogs with advice for entrepreneurs who are starting their own businesses. I'm citing only three because in my estimation they rate as the top ones.

www.theselfemployed.com, is the creation of Steve Strauss, who I'd unhesitatingly nominate as the guru in this field. His website is loaded with great ideas, tips and valuable information as well as links for the newbie business owner.

Strauss also writes a column for *USA Today* and maintains another website there — **www.usatoday.com/money/columnist/strauss/index**. Most of the material there is different than on his website for the self-employed. Check both.

Another website offering substantial how-to advice is maintained by SCORE, formerly known as the Service Corps of Retired Executives, thus the acronym SCORE.

SCORE is a nonprofit organization which offers free business mentoring services, mostly to small business entrepreneurs. It also provides seminars and training. You'll find them located in most mid-sized and larger metro areas throughout the United States. Their website: **www.score.org**.

Since most SCORE mentors are volunteer retired executives, you might encounter a conventional point of view. However, I see no problem with that because even though most of us are more inclined toward the survival approach, i.e. cutting costs and saving money at every turn, we can nevertheless learn a tremendous amount from these experienced volunteers.

66.

Don't Buy Franchises or Existing Businesses

No matter how sweet the offer, beware of businesses that are advertised for sale.

My wife, Sondra, who was an independent businesswoman for most of her adult life, says she cannot remember seeing a viable business offered for sale either in print or online. That's a strong statement.

But, it's one that with rare exception I've found to be true.

She points out that if a business which is being considered for sale is a money maker, then it should work the other way around — prospective buyers approach the business owner, asking if he or she might be interested in selling their business.

On the occasions that I investigated the potential for small businesses that were advertised for sale, I left each time saying to myself that I wouldn't want to take over the business even if it were offered for free.

Some of the circumstances surrounding these businesses were downright sad. I felt empathy for the sellers, most of whom found themselves financially on the edge of a cliff.

I find buying a franchise even more foreboding. First, you must pay upfront a franchise fee which in many instances exceeds $100,000. Then you'll be handed a set of rules for maintaining the franchise chain's standards. I realize that this may be necessary to maintain quality, but the upfront payment combined with numerous restrictions is sufficiently off-putting to keep me away.

The only exception to these negatives that I can recall is the case of my relative, who worked as a mechanic in a small auto repair shop for 20 years. He was approached by his boss who wanted to retire and was considering putting the business up for sale. The owner said that since he had no children, he'd be pleased if my relative bought the business. He even offered to turn it over to him with no money down. He'd only need to make monthly payments. In that instance, my relative had almost as good a knowledge as the owner of the state of the business and its future prospects. However, take note the business was not *advertised* for sale.

Best to start your own business from scratch with no capital outlay and no one else to answer to.

> **Do not wait; the time will never be 'just right.' Start where you stand, and work with whatever tools you may have at your command, and better tools will be found as you go along.**
>
> ***– George Herbert***

67.

When You Need an Expert

When it's really important that you have the right information or advice going forward, you'll need to find an expert.

And I can tell you from experience that there exists on this planet an expert for anything and everything.

The challenge is to find that person when you need him or her.

People needing cataract surgery should seek out an eye surgeon who's done thousands of cataract operations. You don't want the surgeon fresh out of residency. The same principle holds true when you're seeking business advice.

My wife once bought a painting for fifty cents at a thrift store, and it took us six months to find an expert who identified it as the work of a well-known Canadian artist active in the 1940s and 1950s. We ended up selling it at a handsome price.

There are many experts. If, for example, you have a farm that you want to trade for shares in a limited partnership in some offshore oil rigs, someone at the IRS can answer your accountant's most detailed questions about tax consequences in this specific area.

There are medical experts around the world who have based their careers on the study of one particular disease or disorder and they're widely published in professional journals. These are the experts you or your physician may need to contact if you have such a medical problem.

You'll have important questions about your new business and you'll need answers for them.

It's possible that you'll find an expert in your own town or city. Or you might need to launch an Internet search.

You'd be surprised to know that during a routine conversation with a customer, one might say, "You know, I'd like to do this project, but I need some information that I haven't been able to get."

I usually respond by saying that I understand the difficulty, and I'd like to try to find an expert for them, someone with both the background and authority to provide an answer to their question.

I'll sometimes do a search for the customer on my own time and if I'm lucky enough to strike pay dirt, I'll have a grateful customer.

Naturally, I do the same for myself and my own business routinely.

When it counts, I always seek the expert. You should, too.

> **You need to overcome the tug of people against you as you reach for high goals.**
>
> ***– George S. Patton***

68.

Are You Google Savvy?

There's no doubt that the Google search engine can be used effectively to both make money and save money.

The same has been said about social media and social networking. However, I'm not ready to endorse them. I'm skeptical as to whether the investment of your time is justified by the actual payback, assuming that there is one.

You may find it unsettling that I keep bringing up this same issue of the value of your time. However, without being constantly aware and conscious of this critical element, you can easily drift off course.

I urge you to limit time spent online to only those essential duties related to your business. Someday, if you find yourself in fat city and burdened by having too much money in the bank, you might take some time off to play electronic games or learn what your high school classmates are doing now.

Meanwhile, regarding your business startup, you want to pay attention to what is called SEO or search engine optimization.

If you live in Kalamazoo, Michigan and your business is porcelain refinishing of bathtubs and wash basins, you want to make sure that if someone in your city enters "porcelain refinishing" and "Kalamazoo" into Google that your business pops up on the first page. That's what's meant by SEO.

To accomplish that, you'll need someone with expertise in SEO. This is not a tall order. If you don't know someone who has a teenage son or daughter who is familiar with SEO, then contact your local computer group or society and request a recommendation of an SEO expert. There's at least one of these in almost every American city or town.

The advice and service is usually a one-time expense, and is essential to being competitive. The fee should be modest. If someone quotes you a high fee, move on.

If you can't find someone with SEO experience, then search online. The expert needn't be located where you live.

Of course, all of this is predicated on the assumption that you already have a modest website in place.

> **Money lost, nothing lost;**
> **courage lost, everything lost.**
>
> ***– Yiddish saying***

69.

eBay, Etsy and Craigslist

Another way to supplement your income can come from selling items on eBay.com, Etsy.com and Craigslist.org.

Please note that the following suggestions aren't the same as those in Chapter 52 which exclusively focus on establishing a *regular online business* on eBay.

Instead, these tips are aimed primarily at the casual seller who has some items he or she wishes to sell much the same as if he or she were going to hold a garage sale.

On eBay you can offer for sale almost anything, new or used. There are very few exceptions.

You have a choice of offering the item on auction or on Buy It Now for a fixed price. If the item is sold, eBay takes a small commission. If it isn't sold, you owe nothing.

There are some individuals who make a living selling on eBay, but for most it's a sideline.

Some other sellers prefer to use Craigslist, which allows you to place electronic classified ads in your community free of charge.

Etsy is designed for mostly home-based sellers who produce sale items, including art, clothing, etc. that you might expect to see displayed at an arts and crafts fair.

And while Etsy in some instances provides sellers with a living income, it's not something you'd want to count on for a living.

However, you can join the thousands of part-timers who enjoy making extra money selling their handcrafts, vintage items or art.

Unless you have access to certain items that warrant establishing an online business, save eBay, Etsy and Craigslist for your off hours, and reserve your prime time for building your business or for temporary or part-time work that earns you a paycheck.

And if you're in the process of getting rid of some of your unwanted possessions or are cleaning your attic, be cautioned that selling gold, silver or other valuables is a risk because they are your protection against the possibility of double-digit inflation in the future. Also, keep in mind that these assets are easily moved and can be quickly converted to cash if you find yourself in a financial emergency.

> **You must take action now that will move you towards your goals. Develop a sense of urgency in your life.**
>
> ***– H. Jackson Brown, Jr.***

70.

Rx for Bureaucratic Slowness

One of the most memorable movie scenes I recall came from an adaptation of Kafka's *The Trial.*

I use this inspiration whenever I have to deal with bureaucracy or red tape either in business or government.

In the movie, a tired, middle-aged man enters a dark cavernous structure filled with hundreds of long tables. He makes his way through the labyrinth to where a white-bearded attorney in a rumpled black suit sits behind one of the tables.

The audience is subtly informed that the man has been paying this same visit every day for the last 18 years.

We hear the man ask, "How is my case coming along?" The lawyer speaks not one word of dialog. He only nods.

The visitor then takes his briefcase and departs.

Whenever I think I'm getting the run-around in corporate or government offices — whether it's about an application, a pending refund or an order I placed — I pose the tired man's question to the paper-shufflers who answer the phone.

"How's my case coming along?" I ask.

I always request to speak to the same person (that's very important) and I'm always extra polite, if not apologetic. However, I remain persistent to the extreme.

If you phone every day or two, but remain friendly and polite, your respondent will have no legitimate reason to complain to her supervisor about your persistence.

She will decide sooner or later that it's easier to do what has to be done to satisfy you than to keep answering your phone calls.

Not once since I began doing this 15 years ago has anyone asked me, "Case? What case?"

And it almost always works.

71.

The Best Person to Ask for a Loan

There's someone you can always borrow from without paperwork or hassles.

And this person will never ask when you'll pay it back.

Who could this be, you ask?

It's you.

Here's how it works: You open a certificate of deposit (CD) at a bank or credit union. If a few months later you find yourself with a serious need for cash but don't have it on hand and you don't want to apply for a loan, this is what you do. Contact the bank or credit union and tell them that you want to borrow let's say $10,000 on your $25,000 CD.

Within an hour, you can pick up your check. No questions asked, no qualifying, no nothing. You just make the request and the money is there waiting for you.

In most circumstances the bank or credit union will allow you to borrow up to 90 percent of the amount of your CD. You'll continue receiving interest on the CD and there is no payback date. You can make partial or full payments on the loan at any time you wish. Or you can make no payments at all, and when the CD matures, the principal amount of the loan plus accumulated interest will be deducted and you'll receive the balance remaining.

When borrowing on your CD, normally you'll be charged an interest rate of approximately two to three percent above the rate that you're currently receiving on your CD.

The sooner you pay back the loan, the sooner you stop being charged interest.

I used this strategy to maximum advantage for several years before and after the 2008 economic nosedive. My credit union was offering 6.5 percent per year interest on a 7-year CD. That was in 2006. For the next seven years I had the option to borrow my own money at a rate of 9.5 percent while my savings continued to draw 6.5 percent.

Meanwhile, interest rates had fallen to below one percent, but I remained locked in at the contract rate of 6.5 percent.

Often, when I had a large unanticipated expense, I would phone the credit union and within hours the amount I requested would be transferred into my money market account from which I could then write a check.

As soon as I accumulated the payback amount, usually within a period of a few months, I'd return the loaned amount, having paid interest for only that brief period.

Remember, though, it's not a good idea to lock your savings into a 7-year CD at the low rates prevailing at the time I write this. One percent is not an attractive rate to be stuck with for seven years or for any length of time beyond a year or two.

Finally, if you have a CD and wish to borrow on it, first ask a friendly teller for two figures: 1) What would the total interest be if you didn't pay back the loan until the maturity date and (2) What would be the cost to you if you withdrew the money today instead of borrowing it and just paid the applicable penalty. Sometimes, especially if your CD is near the maturity date, it can be cheaper to pay the penalty than to pay interest on the loan.

Check these factors before you make a decision.

72.

Recession-Proof and Export-Proof Businesses

Recently, I watched a late night discussion on TV in which a panel of Stanford University graduate students discussed their futures. One of their prime concerns was finding employment or starting businesses that were both recession-proof and export-proof. They didn't want to invest their time in endeavors that could be shipped overseas and put them out of work.

For example, radiologists are aware that many medical facilities now send x-rays and other medical images to locations such as India for overnight reading and return. They send them as email attachments and get the work done for a fraction of the cost they'd be charged by a physician in the U.S.

As for jobs lost due to the recession or what the spinners and cheerleaders prefer to call "the slow recovery," seldom a day goes by when one doesn't read about a major employer cutting several thousand jobs.

Undoubtedly, some of you reading this have been among those laid off due to plant closures and jobs being shipped overseas.

Given these realities, how do you avoid these pitfalls? The answer might lie with starting your own businesses and working for yourself — not for someone or some company that can end your employment overnight simply by moving a pin on a map at a corporate headquarters located in a distant city.

But just deciding that you wish to be self-employed is only the beginning. You'll need to find a niche business that fills a current need, is without much competition and can't be provided by offshore sources.

At the moment, I know several self-employed individuals whose businesses are both recession-proof and export-proof.

One of these is a man who installs telephone, TV and an assortment of audio-visual cabling inside homes and businesses, including cables for landline telephones. Most communications giants don't want to take up technician time doing any kind of cable installations in homes. If you insist, sometimes they'll quote you a prohibitive hourly fee, which they know you won't want to pay.

So people call my friend, he does the work for a fraction of what the corporations would charge and still makes a good living.

Another friend is a computer guru who comes to your home if your computer is down or not functioning properly. He commands a good hourly fee, but one that is affordable.

I also know an independent heating and air-conditioning technician who specializes in repairing and servicing older equipment. He has little competition from large appliance dealers who primarily want to sell new units and provide service during the warranty period because that's where their profit is highest. When you live in a place like Tucson, repair of an A/C unit during the summer months is *not* discretionary. You either pay to get it fixed or you suffer.

None of these three individuals have any concerns about either a recession or having their jobs shipped overseas.

Each also has a large list of loyal customers whom they treat right, meaning that they would never attempt to overcharge them on fees. Even if they lose a portion of their customer base due to normal attrition, they'll continue to make a decent living and will be adding new customers all the time.

Some additional advice: Stay away from fads and bubbles. Concentrate on the "meat and potatoes" occupations. People will always need to drive their cars, deal with computer problems and keep from freezing in the cold or sweating in the heat.

How many such basic services can you think of? Find the one for which you have training, talent or a strong desire to establish yourself. And if you need additional ideas or inspiration, you can find them in *555 Ways to Earn Extra Money* by Jay Conrad Levinson in paperback via many used book websites. These include betterworldbooks.com, abebooks.com and amazon.com.

> **A successful man is one who can lay a firm foundation with the bricks others have thrown at him.**
>
> ***– David Brinkley***

73.

Spreading the Risk

You're already aware that many self-employed individuals operate several small and often unrelated businesses.

This option can increase your chances of finding both economic stability and security.

Suppose you're doing computer repair and installation and you encounter a slow period. You can benefit from a second or a third business that will help keep you busy during those slow periods.

You might find related businesses such as web design or maintenance or setting up programs for commercial customers.

Admittedly this can sometimes lead to a juggling act, but if you're skilled at deftly handling a crunch, you'll be able to schedule customers according to the urgency of their need and not have to turn away any business.

You can always pare down the sideline businesses if it becomes apparent that one particular business is keeping you busy beyond the normal workload.

But at the start, multiple businesses can be your ticket to sustaining yourself and your family.

An added tip: Have separate business cards printed for each of your small businesses. And you don't need to spend a lot of money. Shop online for cheap business card printing and then check those prices against the local outlets of chain office supply giants.

74.

Beware of the Cheerleaders

I'm not referring here to the high-energy cadres of team spiritboosters at sports events. Instead, the cheerleaders to watch out for are the rah-rah personal finance magazines and other publications that offer retirement and investment advice.

First, it seems they generally avoid writing about the one out of seven Americans who have lost their jobs through no fault of their own.

Instead they prefer to focus on those readers who are high-earning and secure in their jobs.

They all seem to follow a mantra that requires that all investments for retirement should be in securities — a strategy which I find to be heavily dependent on luck.

My own strategy: Pay off your house and all other debts, invest only in quality income property and buy for cash instead of taking a mortgage if you can. Keep only enough cash to see you through emergencies. I believe that America will experience more economic crises in the future and that these will be accompanied by equally severe dislocations. Being prepared for this places you one step ahead of the masses.

Choose a financially conservative path such as this, and you can avoid hard times and the struggle that accompanies such periods.

Certainly you know others who are currently traveling, spending and having a good time while you might be buying the kids clothes at thrift outlets.

It's much like the fable of the grasshopper and the ants. The grasshopper believed he could afford to frolic throughout the late summer and fall while the ants were busy preparing for the winter.

When those future economic downturns occur and things worsen, you'll be sitting comfortably — much like the fabled ants, perhaps in a dated house and driving a ten-year-old car. But unlike your friends, you won't have to be worrying how you are going to meet your mortgage payment or cover your bills. That's consistent with The Survival Mindset which you will read about in Chapter 92.

> **Either you run the day or the day runs you.**
>
> ***– Jim Rohn***

75.

Trade with Small Business

Whenever possible, I prefer to do business with what I call "real people." I try to avoid the corporations and chains where often you don't see the same employee twice.

The individual, the self-employed, the owners of small companies will recognize you as a valued customer when you walk in the door. The same with small, local banks.

The big corporations don't care about you. For them, you are simply a number. Same goes for their employees.

Also, these same corporations and banks always can be counted on to impose the highest fees and service charges.

Can you remember a time when you told an employee at the branch location of a national banking chain that you have been an account holder for 25 years and that perhaps you deserved a little extra consideration regarding a particular issue or concern? If you got more than a blank stare, I'd say you did quite well. As a rule, the larger the business, the less likely your loyalty will be acknowledged, much less rewarded. Admittedly, there are exceptions.

Stay local. Do business with real people. You'll benefit and so will your community.

76.

The Model Entrepreneur

Undoubtedly, the most impressive entrepreneur that I've ever met has probably never received an iota of publicity and has never achieved fame.

We're all familiar with names like Steve Jobs, Bill Gates and Warren Buffet, but the man I'm going to tell you about is both my role model and hero.

Why? Because he's one of us. A little guy who's made it because he believed he could.

My wife and I met this man at a wedding reception. He was in his early thirties and was introduced to us as the manager of a corporate branch office where the bridegroom was employed.

I can attest that this man was not swimming in money at the time and likely earned no more than a simple living from his full-time job.

But, when he told us what he did with his time outside work, it caused my jaw to drop. I wished at the time that I had a pen and notebook because I wanted to write down everything he said.

For starters, he told us that he had recently bought a small farm outside of town. He sold his house in town to help make the down payment and subsequently moved with his family to the farm.

The property came with a good-sized barn, so during the winter months he rented out space inside for boat storage where he sheltered a dozen pleasure crafts for individual owners.

In the summer months, he placed picnic tables under the trees and made them available for family outings.

He set up a roadside stand where he sold his orchard fruits and vegetables and provided u-pick-em opportunities for those who wished to pick their own.

His wife canned fruits and vegetables and made jams to sell.

Next, he planned to open a bed and breakfast for city dwellers who sought to spend a weekend or holiday on a farm.

There was also mention of pony rides for the kids and professional photos to go along.

And there were plans to create a bucolic, hillside venue for weddings and other family events.

We spoke with this man for only about 15 minutes. But, when we returned home we continued to talk about him and his entrepreneurial spirit and to this day we often think about him when entrepreneurial superlatives are mentioned.

What he achieved in such a short period of time convinces me that there are dozens of ancillary income possibilities related to most commercial endeavors. We need only identify and actualize these as did the young entrepreneur we met at the wedding.

> **March on. Do not tarry. To go forward is to move toward perfection. March on, and fear not the thorns, or the sharp stones on life's path.**
>
> ***– Khalil Gibran***

77.

Even if You Are Rehired

If you should be so fortunate to land another job that pays as well as the one you lost, don't make the mistake of feeling too secure.

These are not secure times. So while you should give your new employer an honest day's work, you will play it smart if you continue building your own business during your off hours and on weekends.

The Wall Street Journal recently featured an article about some workers who positioned themselves ahead of the curve in this context. The *Journal* called them "defensive entrepreneurs" because each had prepared for the possibility of layoff or downsizing by establishing his or her own part-time business operated from home.

Their common goal was to expand their businesses to the point where the business could someday support them. Meanwhile, should the ax fall, these part-time entrepreneurs would have a job and an income, albeit a modest income, while they either seek another position or grow their part-time businesses into full-time operations.

Remember, if you were a victim of downsizing, it could happen again. Be smart and protect yourself.

78.

The Power of "Thank You"

Saying "thank you" can pay huge dividends when you're in business, especially in these times when good manners and expressions of gratitude are on the decline.

"Thank you" notes have landed me customers, helped cut through red tape, accelerated approval for a project — or just brought a smile to someone who was pleasantly surprised to receive such a note.

Let me share with you a personal experience on this topic that I'll never forget. I had been invited to a New Year's Eve party by a young woman with whom I was distantly acquainted through a hiking club. I was unmarried at the time and had no plans for New Year's Eve. So, when I received a phone call inviting me to attend her party, I accepted immediately although I was virtually a stranger to the hostess and her guests.

The party was convivial, but uneventful and I departed shortly after the New Year was ushered in. The next day, I routinely mailed a note card to the hostess, thanking her for inviting me to her party.

Several weeks later, I encountered the hostess in a supermarket. After a few words of small talk, she mentioned my card, adding that it was the first "Thank you" card she'd ever received.

I was dumbfounded. This woman was in her early thirties, educated, a professional woman — and this was the first time in her life that she had received a written expression of thanks? It caused me to realize the importance of a "Thank you" card and the impact that it can make.

Another related experience came when I was employed at the Miami Department of Publicity and Tourism and after I had given a brief tour of Miami to a visiting tourism official from a smaller city at the request of my boss. After the visitor returned home, I received a letter which I have kept to this day. Typed on his official letterhead were these words: "Thanks, George. I hope I can be so kind to you sometime." The entire body of the letter consisted of only that *one line* of type.

That single line really stood out, and the example has served me well. I have used that same message for my own "Thank you" letters numerous times.

Sending a "Thank You" card or note requires so little effort. But, it sets you apart from others and can be one of the best investments you'll ever make.

A final tip: Go out and buy a small box of "Thank You" cards. No, make that two boxes! Use them liberally.

Anytime you have reason to express your appreciation to anyone who helps you in your business or provides a lead to other work, get a "Thank You" card in the mail right away. It will make someone's day.

79.

Be a Joiner

Anyone who plans to succeed in business must be a joiner. This doesn't mean that you must commit yourself to a large number of organizations and never miss a meeting.

It does mean that you need to be a social animal. You want to build a reputation as someone who makes a contribution to the community.

You know the old saying, "What goes around comes around," and more recently "Pay it forward." Well, it's true. And not only will community service advance your business prospects, but it will give you a good feeling because of what you are doing to improve your community and the quality of life of all who live there.

These opportunities include religious affiliations, business and service clubs such as Kiwanis, Lions, Rotary, Sertoma and a long list of others. There are also local computer groups, historical societies, sports-related clubs including hiking, hunting, fishing, bowling and many others. Add to that neighborhood improvement associations and homeowner association boards of directors.

The more organizations you join the greater your opportunities for exposure of your business and making contacts. But you can't jump into every organization with both feet. If you do, you won't have any time to run your business.

One rule of thumb is to ferret out which organizations are flexible when it comes to attendance and participation as there are some that will drop you if miss a certain number of meetings.

Many, however, are just happy to have you on their membership rolls and welcome another dues-paying member. And if you can attend a meeting every now and then, as your work schedule permits, you'll remaining in good standing.

80.

How to Win Friends

You might have seen *How to Win Friends and Influence People* by Dale Carnegie on your parents' bookshelf.

First published in 1936 and translated into dozens of languages, 15 million copies have been sold to date. This paperback book has been updated and is still selling copies all over the world as you read this.

To be honest, I didn't realize the importance of the book until I started my own business. What I'd learned from life experience plus what I gained from the book helped set me on the path to a better way of life.

You can buy a used paperback copy online for as low as $1.00.

I cannot stress often enough that success in your own small business depends not only in offering your customers quality merchandise or outstanding service, but on how you relate to the customer.

People skills and communication skills should not be underestimated, especially in the role they will play in your business future.

81.

Beating the Traffic

If you live in a metropolitan area with traffic congestion during the rush hours and beyond, here's a tip for saving you many hours of downtime waiting in traffic.

When customers phone you and ask you to come to their office, shop or plant for a service call or a meeting and would like you to come the next day or as soon as possible, you need to be ready with a prepared response.

When I was in business in the Silicon Valley, the conversation often went like this:

"George, can you come to our office tomorrow morning at 8 o'clock?"

"Just a moment, let me check my calendar. Yes, I can meet with you tomorrow morning, but I already have an early morning appointment. Could we meet at 10 a.m.?"

If the answer was "yes," no problem. We met at 10 a.m.

But, if a 10 a.m. meeting wasn't possible for my customer, I would advise him/her that I was available on the following morning, also at 10 a.m. And also the next day at 10 a.m.

Why was that 10 a.m. time so important to me? If I accepted an 8 a.m. or a 9 a.m. appointment time it meant that I would need to add a couple of hours to the time I would be away from my home office, most of which would be burned up inching along in freeway traffic.

I knew that the peak rush-hour periods in the Silicon Valley began at 6 a.m. and continued through 9 or 9:30 a.m. The afternoon rush hour began at 1 p.m. and continued through 6 or 6:30 p.m.

So, making a 10 a.m. appointment was the only sure-fire time that would keep me from wasting almost a half a day stuck in traffic.

Although this strategy amounted to a white lie, it was nevertheless a survival tool, one of many that helped keep me afloat.

And I can happily report that over many years, I can't remember a time when a customer showed annoyance over my request to shift or adjust appointment times.

Apropos this issue, there are a couple of other helpful hints for saving time.

One is to familiarize yourself not only with peak period traffic on freeways, but also to know which city streets you can use to avoid delays and when is the best time to use them.

For example, where I live now, I've found that many workers are due to report to work at 8 a.m. If I use city streets between 7:30 and 8 a.m., I will encounter heavy traffic on the main thoroughfares. However, if I depart from my house exactly at 8 a.m., I find that vehicular traffic has been reduced by more than half. The obvious reason is that all of the workers who were due to report at 8 a.m. have arrived at their places of employment and those who have 8:30 or 9 a.m. starting times haven't yet left their driveways.

Another tip is to use a courier service for certain needs, especially when a large envelope or parcel needs to be delivered to your customer ASAP.

Rather than deliver it yourself using your own car and encountering traffic delays and loss of time, hire a courier service to deliver it. Usually, the costs are nominal and delivery is made either the same day or early the next.

82.

Never Litigate... Except

When I was a newspaperman, I covered civil courts full time for more than eight years. If I learned one thing from that experience it was *never litigate.*

The cost of litigating is guaranteed to drain you both of funds and energy. You can't afford this, so don't even consider it. Whatever it is that you want to sue about, let it go. Even if you're a winner in court, you will be a loser because of what is taken from you by virtue of being embroiled in a lawsuit.

There is only one exception to this admonition. If you are injured in an accident and there is a liability issue, you can safely proceed with litigation *if*— and it's an important *if*— if an attorney will agree to take your case on contingency. This means the lawyer will take the case for a percentage of the final judgment or settlement as his or her fee. You are not required to pay any money up front and pay only the agreed percentage if the attorney prevails in securing compensation for your damages and/or injuries.

Most often, an attorney will not accept a case on contingency unless he/she is virtually certain of recovering some compensation for you.

There are few other types of civil cases that an attorney will accept on contingency. Some among those are product liability cases or slip-and-fall accidents.

Like many other admonitions that you have already read in this book, this goes back to the value of your time. If you are spending time in court or brooding over some injustice that has been done you, this is time that you are not spending building your business. You must keep focused and not allow anything other than your family's health emergencies or a leaking roof to distract you.

It is worthy of mention here to note that there exists a major distinction between litigating and seeking advice from an attorney. By all means, I strongly recommend that you consult an attorney/expert before proceeding in any area of business where uncertainty exists. In fact, a consultation with an attorney/expert can save you money and stress that you absolutely don't need at this time in your life. However, be sure that the attorney you are consulting is an expert on the specific subject of your concern. You wouldn't consult a podiatrist if you are having severe headaches.

> **Things do not happen. Things are made to happen.**
>
> ***– John F. Kennedy***

83.

Risk Management is Key

Although in Chapter 64 we tangentially touched on the issue of risk management, there's much more.

Risk management must always be in the forefront of your calculations and decisions.

In addition to invoking the decision-making strategies used over a half-century ago by President John Kennedy and his inner circle, you also need the ability to factor in the dollars and cents mathematics that will enable you to decide whether to go forward with an idea for expanding your business or buying new equipment, etc.

Though it's not as complicated as you might think, there are certain elements that need to be brought into the picture.

And while it's impossible to list here every possible index and consideration, let me offer just a few.

Suppose you are considering buying new equipment. Price shouldn't be your only consideration. Search not only Consumer Reports, but also use Google's search engine to take you to online sellers whose websites also include buyer reviews of the product. Those comments from both satisfied and dissatisfied buyers provide me with a treasure trove of information. Another critical factor often covered by Consumer Reports is frequency of repair. You can't afford to buy a piece of equipment that requires frequent repair.

And, of course, you must factor in the expected life of the product.

Maybe you're considering another startup. What capital or expense is needed to begin? How long will it take to find out if the new business is viable and how much time and money do you stand to lose in a worst case scenario?

The upshot of this is that no matter what the risk issue under discussion, the best way to approach it is as you would a dress rehearsal for a play.

Line up all the pertinent factors, invite your spouse and your inner circle of friends to join you and spend a few hours running through the "dress rehearsal." Encourage questions, challenges and alternative suggestions.

Using whatever tools are at your disposal, work the issue at hand until it's figuratively ready to drop and there's nothing further left to ask or talk about.

In the end, you might find that the risk isn't justified and you scuttle the idea. In such a case, you still come out a winner because you've been spared the loss of time and money invested.

> **It is no use saying, 'We are doing our best.' You have got to succeed and do what is necessary.**
>
> ***– Winston Churchill***

84.

The Importance of Character

If you're going to own and manage a business, you need to hone your ability to judge character. Mistakes in this area you truly cannot afford.

At the risk of overwriting on this subject, I must tell you that in my lifetime the most damaging and costly decisions I've made and later regretted involved errors in character judgment. I would hope that what you read here will help you to avoid making similar mistakes.

In whatever field I found myself dealing with others, I always made it a point to filter out those individuals with whom I felt uncomfortable working. Those remaining were the "keepers," and I counted on them to treat me right.

Initially, although I could often screen out someone upon first meeting, it often required a trial run on a project where they couldn't do much damage or overcharge me. Those first small jobs that I handed to a new-to-me tradesperson were in fact "auditions."

After disassociating myself from those about whom I had doubts or suspicions — I never fire anyone — I just don't call them back to do another job, I focused my attention on the three or four tradespersons whom I then felt I could trust.

Today, I still work with three tradesmen with whom I began working 25 years ago. In that time, I've never had to question a bill and they have never had to wait for payment. This to me is part of what I consider my security and perhaps the reverse might hold true for them. Everything we do is done on a handshake. There are no forms to fill out and I don't ask for bids.

There are several traits which you can observe that might help you to avoid individuals who can prove to be bad news. Among these are observing how people dress and carry themselves.

Do they exhibit good manners? Do you feel they are listening to what you have to say? What kind of an appearance would they present if introduced to one of your customers?

What type of vehicle are they driving? Is it a flashy or expensive sports car? Does the person manifest altruistic qualities or does he/she appear self-centered?

If it's another small business owner or someone working for a middle size or large company with whom you might be doing business, are they members of the Better Business Bureau? Always a good sign. If they are or not, you can check out their complaint record with the Better Business Bureau by going online.

While this all perhaps doesn't tell you specifically how to judge character, I can suggest a simple procedure referred to earlier in this chapter. That is to take a page out of the playbook of most employers — both large and small — who almost never hire anyone full time to start or engage them in a large or long-term project. Instead, to avoid firing or potential lawsuits, they hire people either temporary or part time or take a baby step by contracting for a small project, one that would carry no repercussions if it wasn't done right. If they don't work out, they aren't fired, but informed that the temporary work has ended and they might be called back in the future if something opens up.

Meanwhile, those who are found to be suitable are asked to fill the first full-time opening that occurs. They have already been vetted on the job, which is a much more reliable predictor than what's on a resume or said during a brief interview.

The same applies to vendors or others with whom you might do business. There is now a track record established and there is a greater likelihood that they will perform well in the future.

Whether you wish to engage the person to remodel your kitchen, house-sit when you're away, undertake some major repairs or babysit, you need to have a good feeling about who you're hiring. If there's any doubt, it should be a no go.

If you feel you haven't yet honed your character judging skills, ask a friend whose judgment you trust to be present with you when you interview.

When you are interviewing, ask questions, request references, and don't sign anything or announce your decision immediately. Say that you need to talk with your spouse or partner and that you will get back to them shortly.

Use the Internet to do a Google search. If it's a person who holds a medical license, check the website of your state's board of medical examiners to determine if there has been any disciplinary action. Often you will find websites where customers or patients have submitted reviews. Read them.

As noted in Chapter 102, in most communities the best know the best. A lawyer specializing in real estate law will usually know who's the best tax lawyer in town. A top orthopedic surgeon can point you to the best physical therapist.

But you can't always count on that. A few years ago, I needed to undergo a minor hernia repair and I began by asking around among some of our friends in the medical field. One of them gave me the name of a general surgeon. When I looked him up on the state's Board of Medical Examiners website under the disciplinary records, I found that he had a rap sheet as long my arm.

That's why I urge both due diligence and redundancy when it really counts.

This also includes checking online with the Better Business Bureau and other sources such as the state's contractor's licensing authority, court records and your local newspaper's archives.

Don't rely on just one source. Check and double check and then triple check until you're satisfied that there are no other places left to investigate. Discuss your decision with your spouse and your inner circle.

We're not talking about whether you should or shouldn't decide to buy a box of cookies from the Girl Scouts. The kind of serious vetting that I've outlined above is for when it really counts. When you've got something on the line where you can't afford to take an unnecessary risk.

Take nothing for granted. We're living in a different age. It's not what it was when your parents and grandparents lived in small towns where business was done on a handshake and people left their doors unlocked at night.

Stay alert and reduce your chances of becoming a victim.

A failure is not always a mistake, it may simply be the best one can do under the circumstances. The real mistake is to stop trying.

– B. F. Skinner

85.

The Well-Connected Know the Way

In my lifetime, I have encountered a number of individuals who I found to have impeccable credentials when it comes to being "well-connected."

For those of you who haven't served in the military, we're referring to a type of man or woman who can get things done when no one else can. Or they can ferret out information when everyone else fails.

Remember the role played by Morgan Freeman in the epic movie *The Shawshank Redemption*? He was in a limited sense "well-connected."

Earlier in my life, a shipmate told me about another sailor he encountered who was known as "Angles" Brown. That wasn't his real surname, of course. According to my buddy, if you needed a pass for a long weekend ashore or if you lacked an extra replacement for an item that was a part of your uniform or just had a hankering for a hamburger outside of mealtime hours, "Angles" could get it for you. There was a "service charge" added, of course.

Even if you wanted to get a transfer to a Caribbean duty station or to Hawaii, "Angles" could help arrange it.

"Angles" was well-connected and a very useful man to know.

It will be in your interest to connect with someone like this.

But, take note that I'm not suggesting that you connect with anyone who operates on the wrong side of the law. Absolutely to the contrary. Avoid such individuals as they are certain to get you in trouble. Also, I would advise not getting too cozy with your contact. Instead maintain a cordial, but arm's length relationship. Such a person acts more as a limited advisor or agent to fill certain needs, but shouldn't be considered a pal or a member of your team.

My definition of a well-connected person is a law-abiding individual who is plugged in to the right places. Someone who can tell you who to avoid and who to approach. Someone who can accurately forecast what's going to happen in six months and why or why not you should invest either your time or money as regards your independent business. Someone who can advise you who to contact at a company where you seek to do business and — more importantly — who to avoid.

This same well-connected person can also advise who you need to cultivate to open a previously-closed door. Example: You take your car to certain garage for gas and service. You get to know the owner/operator. You make small talk every time you go there. You do something nice for him and his workers. You become a regular customer. You already learned from your contact that the gas station owner's brother-in-law is the purchasing agent at the local XYZ Corp. A good word about you from the gas station owner to his brother-in-law will pave the way and perhaps open a door that might be otherwise closed to you. As the saying goes, it's often not what you know, but who you know.

These are not guarantees that you will get the business nor is there any hint or suggestion of behind-the-scenes scheming, bribery or wrongdoing. What it does mean is that these little breaks combined with you being personable help to open doors for you. Once that door has been opened, you will need to stand on your own merits.

Where I live now, I enjoy having lunch with a friend who can qualify for the title of not only well-connected but also well-informed at least five times over. I leave these lunches having learned of what are usually more new consumer money-saving opportunities than I ever dreamed existed as well as behind-the-scenes information about what's going on in the community.

Many of his great tips are included in the money-saving section of this book.

Where do you have the best chance of meeting well-connected individuals?

You are most likely to encounter such individuals at networking meetings or gatherings such as the breakfast group I described in Chapter 5.

These folks usually are familiar with survival strategies as they have often come up that way themselves and seem more amenable to helping others.

> **Find a way to say yes to things.**
> **Say yes to invitations to a new country,**
> **say yes to meet new friends,**
> **say yes to learn something new.**
>
> ***– Eric Schmidt***

86.

Barter Your Skills

If you or a member of your family possess any special skills, in addition to applying them in an independent business, consider using them to barter.

If you are good at sewing or alterations, cutting hair, auto repair, computer services, web design, language translation to name just a few, you may find neighbors or acquaintances, who like yourself, are not flush with cash and might prefer to trade their specialized services for yours, i.e., barter.

Example, your neighbor cuts your family's hair every month and your teenage son services the neighbor's computers.

Small potatoes? Not worth considering? Think again.

If you're a family of four, those four haircuts would cost a minimum of $60.00 in a low-cost-of-living area and a lot more in a high-cost area.

Wouldn't it be better if you were able to keep that $60.00 in your pocket?

> **Small deeds done are better than great deeds planned.**
>
> ***– Peter Marshall***

87.

Age Discrimination

Even if you are only looking for part-time work in a low-paying job — perhaps something temporary until you can build up your business — take a look around that store or office where you're thinking of applying and check to see how many people over 40 are working there. If you see all young faces, 20- and 30-somethings, don't waste your time filling out an application.

Sure, you can file an age discrimination complaint with a federal agency, but again the need for expedience trumps whatever time and effort you would have to sacrifice to prove you were treated unfairly.

And perhaps after four or five years of delaying action, you *might* get a favorable ruling.

And by that time, it's likely the company would have had time to come up with a legitimate reason for not hiring you.

It's not worth your time. Move on!

> **Determine never to be idle. No person will have occasion to complain of the want of time who never loses any. It is wonderful how much may be done if we are always doing.**
>
> ***– Thomas Jefferson***

88.

Can I Ever Retire?

In an upside down economy, retirement has quickly become a pipe dream for many, especially for those laid off from their jobs during their peak earning periods. And this doesn't include those who have earned what they believed were adequate pensions only to find them insufficiently funded or worse, that they no longer exist.

Social Security is still there, but with the retirement age being increased and considering the modest amount of the monthly payments, one's financial future isn't exactly rosy.

So, what are your alternatives? What is secure nowadays?

Well, there's gold. But the problem with gold is that it's a non-performing asset, meaning that while it holds its value fairly well, it doesn't provide you with any periodic income payments like a stock dividend, annuity, Treasury bond or income property.

The stock market? In recent years it's been a roller coaster. If you can handle the uncertainties, the ups and downs, the risks, then perhaps it might be for you.

Annuities, generally speaking, can't be passed on to your children. There are many restrictions and some unfriendly tax consequences.

Treasury bonds are safe, but if you are holding bonds that are now paying 2.5 percent and if interest rates jump to 7 percent, the value of your bond will decrease and your interest income will remain at 2.5 percent.

And then there's income property. To begin, all income property is not created equal. For example, there is residential property, commercial property and industrial property, also agricultural property.

For me, residential income property has been a lifesaver and enabled a secure retirement for me that I had feared would be impossible after leaving corporate employment.

Short of winning the lottery, I've found this to be the only solid investment that can provide financial security and is within reach of the average individual. It often requires years of hard work and self-discipline, but under most circumstances real estate will protect you against the most drastic economic changes — inflation, recession, stagnation and depression.

My plan was to buy, over a period of several years, four single-family rental houses in addition to the house in which I live, and have them essentially paid off within 20 years.

My first rental house and those that came later were all in solid, middle-class neighborhoods where the houses were well-maintained and showed pride of ownership. I made certain to buy only in stable neighborhoods where there existed few, if any, rental houses.

My standard was to zero-in on properties that would be suitable to rent for a price that a postal employee, teacher or auto mechanic could afford.

I sought to buy the lowest-priced and smallest houses in the best neighborhoods within my price range. And only one-story, single-family houses, preferably situated in a community which is governed by a homeowners association.

Most HOAs will immediately crack down on scofflaw residents who park pickup trucks in the front yards or work on old cars which are on blocks in clear view of passersby. The more "no-nonsense" the HOA, the better for your property values and the more attractive it is to the type of tenants you are seeking.

After buying my first rental house, I became equally as determined to reach the point where I could retire as I was about surviving in my own business. Any extra money that came in was plowed into rental property. I felt that it gave me added security and it kept my taxes low.

And the few times that either my wife or I inherited a modest sum, we postponed home improvements, new cars or vacations and bought a rental house for cash instead. We both preferred adding to our long-term security rather than having the latest model SUV in the driveway.

When you purchase a house as your principal residence, you'll find that you'll have an easier time with financing. Lenders become wary if you declare that you are buying a house with the intent of using it as a rental.

However, after you've lived in your principal residence for a respectable period of time and fixed it up to your satisfaction, there's nothing that prevents you from moving out and turning it into a rental. Normally, under such circumstances, your mortgage rate remains unchanged.

There are numerous books on how to buy and manage rental property. One of my favorites is *Building Wealth One House at a Time* by John W. Schaub (McGraw-Hill). There are many others. Read all you can so you can come away with a consensus.

As you gradually add to your string of rental properties you'll find that you'll have paper losses to report on your income tax return due to negative cash flow and depreciation. You will pay lower income taxes and at the same time see your equity increase. If you're in business for yourself and you're doing well, you'll benefit from these tax shelters which will minimize what you owe the government at year's end.

If you can stay the course for a minimum of 20 years, and pay your mortgages down to little or nil, you should be able to count on receiving one "paycheck" per house per month during your retirement. Each monthly rental income check from your tenants will come close to providing income comparable to your previous weekly salary during your working years.

Of course, a lot depends on where you live and what your earnings were during you highest-pay working years.

If your rentals are, let's say, in San Jose, California, your rental income will be substantially higher than if they are in Pine Bluff, Arkansas.

If double-digit inflation occurs, for example, your rents go up accordingly and your standard of living doesn't suffer. I read recently that 93 percent of all retired people sustain a decline in their standard of living when there is inflation. This underscores why you must be prepared for all eventualities. Otherwise you don't have real security.

More examples: If there's minimum inflation, you don't need major increases in rent. And if there's a depression, you will have little debt — if any — remaining. And that's the key: having your properties *virtually paid off.* That way, in hard times, you can afford to lower the rent on your houses without being hurt while other rental property owners who have high mortgage payments cannot afford to do this.

A few tips about buying a house, whether to live in yourself or use as a rental:

One of the biggest misconceptions about buying a home is that buying a fixer-upper saves you scads of money. Nothing could be farther from the truth. Actually, it will cost you *more* in the long run.

In almost all instances, a buyer is better off waiting for a "Pride of Ownership" property in a desirable neighborhood to come onto the market than falling into the fixer-upper trap.

"Pride of Ownership" houses account for perhaps one in 10 or one in 20 of all resale homes. But they are out there and clearly worth the wait. Your first walk-through tells you that the owners have lovingly cared for the house, performed all needed maintenance, made improvements and upgraded the exterior and landscaping. Ironically, though such houses should bring a premium price, "Pride of Ownership" sellers rarely receive more than the average market price for so-called "comparable" homes in the same neighborhood.

Almost always when you buy a resale house — even though it's *not* a fixer-upper — you'll discover a lot of deferred maintenance that will become your responsibility. Many houses need painting inside and out, new roofs, new carpeting or other floor coverings. All of these items must be added to the cost of the house. However, rarely will the seller reduce the price to cover such expenses. On the other hand, in the case of the "Pride of Ownership" house, you have no such expenses, and yet you pay almost the same price.

How do you calculate the costs needed to bring a house up to par? First, your real estate agent will likely recommend hiring a professional home inspector. These folks usually do a fair job, but to be thorough I suggest hiring your own experts from the trades. These include a heating/air-conditioning technician, a plumbing and electrical expert, a landscaper, a roofing contractor, a licensed pest control operator, a general handyman and sometimes a tree surgeon. Although these experts are among my regular vendors, I always insist on paying each a fee even if they offer to perform the inspection as a courtesy. That's because if they do find a serious deficiency that causes me to exercise my contractual right to cancel the purchase within the inspection period, I want to be able to contact them again to inspect other properties without feeling that each time they need to do it without charge as a favor to me.

Also remember, if the neighboring houses aren't well-maintained, don't buy the house at any price. You can repair and upgrade a house, but you *can't fix the entire neighborhood.* This often comes as a hard-learned lesson for many home buyers.

Should you decide to invest in rental property, you need to know that besides buying the right property, the next most important element is renting to the right tenants and then keeping them. That means screening them for credit history and any other background check that local fair housing laws permit.

These are some requirements that you can include in your advertising and also make a part of the lease: Prohibiting smoking on the property. Requiring a good credit record (not just OK). Requiring in the lease that tenants agree to observe all rules and regulations set down by the HOA.

Once you've found good tenants, reward them by keeping their rents well below market and providing a modest discount for rents paid on or before the first of each month.

There are many other techniques for successful property management. As noted earlier, you can learn a lot in advance by reading books on the subject, but also there are many real estate schools that offer summary courses on property management for the non-professional. Check on these opportunities with your local real estate schools. As for some of the heavily-promoted get-rich-quick real estate seminars that are promoted on TV, I find them expensive and offering no more than courses that are always available in your community for a fraction of the cost.

Finally, I wish to underscore that owning and managing rental property is not for everyone. You need to know in advance exactly what you're getting into and decide what's best for you. Just because it worked for me, doesn't mean that it's suitable for you. Read the recommended books, perform your own due diligence, consult with your trusted advisors and then make your decision.

And one final tip: Avoid getting into commercial property. Today we are seeing more brick and mortar stores and chains going out of business because consumers are increasingly buying online. This does not bode well for the owners of commercial property. Meanwhile, there is less demand for office space because many workers are employed at home and they telecommute between their company's headquarters and often its customers. Residential real estate does not face these same challenges.

Remember, owning and managing rental property is not for everyone.

89.

More About Work-at-Home Offers

As noted earlier in this book, beware of work-at-home offers. These offers appear to fall into three main categories.

The first category is what I consider a legitimate and straightforward one, but unfortunately these are among the few. An example of this category is an airline that allows you to take reservations for the airline's customers from the comfort of your home. Such jobs are rarely advertised and you normally only learn about these by word of mouth from a friend or acquaintance.

If you should come across one of these opportunities, be sure to vet it carefully. It's great to have a full-time or part-time job taking reservations for XYZ Hotels or taking orders for the ABC Corporation. But before you sign on the dotted line make sure that you're not being employed by a middle person rather than by the actual corporation. If it's a middle person, then the corporation is not responsible for paying your salary and has no obligation to you, legally speaking.

And if you are asked to pay *any* fees, upfront or otherwise, bail out immediately, as this is a very bad sign.

The second category is one that is usually an out-and-out flim-flam. You are promised the world, but first you must pay a registration fee or some such. Whatever they wish to call it, it's not for you. Bail out immediately.

The last category is more subtle. You will be asked to bid on a specific job that is usually posted online. You will waste a lot of your time preparing the bid. If your bid is low enough, you might be contacted. If it's high, you're likely not to hear or to be informed that your bid is too high.

In the end, the party that is seeking the bid would like to get you to work for them at slave labor wages, usually well below the minimum wage.

In this category, my advice is don't even spend the time needed to apply. Just skip it and move on to more productive activity, such as promoting your own business.

For those who like statistics, in April, 2014, *Money Magazine* reported that the websites oDesk and eLance, which were scheduled to merge, listed 8 million professionals registered and looking for work, up from 900,000 in 2009. Does that tell you something?

> **Many an opportunity is lost because a person is out looking for four-leaf clovers.**
>
> ***– Anonymous***

90.

Social Programs and Benefits

This chapter may not sit well with everyone, especially those who believe that social programs have no place in our society.

If you are planning to move to another state and do not object to receiving benefits for which you worked and paid during most of your working career, then you might wish to take into consideration some of these factors

If you move to a Blue State, it's more likely that you will find social programs and benefits are most often better than those in Red States.

When I refer to Red States, I have in mind states such as Alabama, Mississippi, Louisiana, South Carolina and Arkansas, those being more politically conservative.

Blue States such as California, Oregon, Washington, Wisconsin, Minnesota, Iowa, Vermont, Massachusetts and others are among those that tend to be more liberal and support a wider range of social programs.

However, it's important to emphasize that rating the quality of a state's social programs is only one part of the mix. There are other considerations that have been noted earlier.

If you have members of your household who are in need of frequent or constant medical care, then this concern and its costs might be a major factor in your choice of a state in which to resettle.

91.

The Problem in Hiring Relatives

A few years ago, a tradesman was at our house doing some work. He was an outgoing individual, so during a break we struck up a conversation.

With a clear sign of frustration on his face, he recounted what appeared to be a painful memory.

"Last year," he said, "I had three trucks out on the street. One of them was driven by my brother-in-law who I hired because he was out of work and needed a job."

"Big mistake!" said the tradesman. "I found I was going around all day fixing and redoing the work of the other two guys. This year, I'm working by myself and making more money."

I have both heard about and seen this occur before. The lesson learned is that it's unwise to hire close friends or relatives simply because they need a job. Even if they are well-qualified, there's a risk because if you need to lay them off it can result in hurt feelings if not the end of a friendship.

As a colleague of mine once said, "Better to make a cash donation — such as 'Here's $______, pay me back when you can.'" — rather than paint yourself into a corner by hiring a relative or a close friend. You should not take on the responsibility for another person's economic welfare at a time when you yourself are trying to get back on your feet.

92.

Adopt a Survival Mindset

By this time you should be familiar with the writings and strategies of Jay Conrad Levinson. If you aren't, I urge you to read his books immediately or you will be missing the heart of what establishing your own economic independence is all about.

In his writings, Levinson focuses on guerrilla marketing and invokes the term "guerrilla mindset." While these words make it clear that it requires an intense and fearless commitment to achieve success, I prefer the term "survival mindset" which I believe best describes what will help us reach our goal.

It's not something that I aspired to do when I first set out in life, but rather it's what I was forced to do to survive. I would have preferred to live in a society where financial stability was not an overriding concern. Where individuals worked mostly from 9 to 5, had weekends and holidays off and took their families on two-week vacations to the mountains or the seashore. Where workers stayed on a single job until they retired and where one-income families were the rule.

Well, that's all gone now with some few exceptions, and you can only read about it in the history books or hear about it from your parents or grandparents.

So, what should you do? Accept the fact that you live in an upside down economy and allow yourself to be tossed onto the junk pile like worn out tires?

Some, who lack the necessary motivation, will indeed fall by the wayside, which is sad. But, *you* won't fall victim to this phenomenon because you've already taken the first step by purchasing this book and reading it this far.

Now, if you haven't already done so, you must adopt a new attitude, and it's what I refer to above as your survival mindset.

You learn how to avoid or surmount obstacles to your financial recovery and ultimate stability. You learn how to fluff off concerns about what your acquaintances or neighbors might think about how you live or dress or what kind of vehicle you drive. You don't allow yourself to be outer-directed by such considerations. You realize that you must be inner-directed, especially as it affects the allocation of your valuable time. Of course, there are exceptions, especially when it comes to your immediate family.

Your survival mindset now tells you that you can get by without buying some discretionary item you really don't need. You learn to turn down invitations to play cards or watch a sporting event at someone's house if you have an opportunity to score points by providing a weekend service to a distressed customer or new prospect when everyone else has turned him down.

Your goal is to reach the point of economic freedom. A point where you will *never again* be subject to the whims of the market or whatever else might influence whether or not you still have a job.

The survival mindset is a powerful tool that will help take you where you want to go.

> **Go for it now.**
> **The future is promised to no one.**
>
> ***– Wayne Dyer***

Part III
How to Save Money

93.

Reduce Fixed Monthly Costs

Although this may seem very obvious, if you haven't already done so, you must absolutely focus on reducing your fixed expenses.

If you can do this — and I realize that there are many people who can't or won't — I urge you to take the medicine and deal with this painful and distasteful chore immediately. As in *today*! Once you've done it, you will certainly sleep better, and you'll be actually doing something to help yourself.

Trust me. Fixed monthly obligations are no small burden. What you can save by eliminating just a few recurring expenses counts for a lot more than finding a bargain or saving money on a purchase.

We recently cut the cord on our satellite TV service because we decided the monthly cost didn't justify what we were getting for our money. We immediately saved a thousand dollars a year.

At the time, I remarked to my wife, "Pay almost a hundred dollars a month to watch commercials? Are you kidding me?"

(There is more about cutting the cord in Chapter 129.)

There are numerous other monthly expenses that can be reduced or completely eliminated. For example, you can do away with your cellphone service's monthly contract and buy a prepaid phone that includes a certain number of prepaid minutes to be used within a specified period. Many cellphone users are paying up to $100 a month for services that might be desirable, but are not essential. You must shop around.

(There is more about saving money on cellphone service in Chapter 146.)

Cutting some of these expenses will be tough decisions. Some family members are likely to howl in protest. If it were my kids who were complaining, my response would be, "It's fine to text if that's the way *you* want to spend *your* money. But, right now there's no money in the family budget for this purpose. So, if texting is that important to you, I'm sure you can find work after school to earn enough to pay for it."

Unfortunately, kids nowadays tend to be more egocentric than in prior decades and although we don't care to admit it, responsibility falls with the parents who have given them too much and asked too little.

If you haven't filed for bankruptcy but are thinking about it, consider using the possibility of bankruptcy as a powerful bargaining chip or lever in negotiating with creditors. You may be able to persuade them that it's in their best interest to reduce your monthly payments or interest rate rather than end up having to take back a house, a car or recreational vehicle.

Chief among those to contact would be your mortgage-holder or lender. Whether it's bankruptcy or foreclosure, just the mention of either usually gets the attention of creditors or lenders.

You need to know for certain whether you will be better off filing for bankruptcy and drastically lowering your credit rating *before* you attempt to negotiate. A good accountant or lawyer should be consulted.

And if you are not in heavy debt on your credit cards and you are considering bankruptcy, be sure to focus on the card where you have the best payment record and try to keep that card up to date with timely payments. Then, should you have to file bankruptcy and end up losing some of your credit cards, you will have one card that you likely will be able to keep and continue to use.

In another part of this book, I emphasize the importance of frugal credit card use.

In all, you'll need to muster the self-discipline to trim all the frills and non-essential expenses from your budget. The less you can get by with the sooner you will reach your goal — solvency and peace of mind.

> **Being frugal does not mean being cheap! It means being economical and avoiding waste.**
>
> ***– Catherine Pulsifer***

94.

Be Debt Free

For many readers, just the mere suggestion of living debt free will provoke a response such as, "Are you kidding me?"

That's probably a reasonable reaction considering that most Americans have not experienced living without debt since reaching majority age. Nor will most be out of debt any time during the remainder of their lives.

The fact is that being in debt has become a way of life.

However, talk to someone who is debt free and you will find a liberated spirit.

I'm one of those, and I can tell you that I don't ever lie awake at night worrying if I can meet my payments. By contrast, imagine those already in debt who must add the worry of losing their jobs.

Beyond mortgage payments on rental properties — I paid those off as quickly as I could — I only once found myself in debt. That was when I was forced to replace an old car which literally fell apart. I paid off a new economy car within six months although the payments were scheduled over a 60-month period. And I drove the car for the next 23 years until its life ended.

You cannot imagine the feeling of independence that being debt free provides. You are under no obligation to anyone. What you have, you own free and clear. No one can take it away.

I also don't borrow money from in-laws or relatives. When you do that, you give them power over your life.

I'm often asked, "Are you saying I should live within my means?"

My answer is, “No, you should live *below* your means.” If you don’t, how are you ever going to be able to set aside money to invest in your retirement?

Some individuals have never thought about retirement. Their concern might only begin when they approach Social Security age. Then, it’s too late to do much about it.

A key element in this survival mindset is not allowing yourself to be influenced by the plethora of ads for consumer goods and gadgets that bombard us.

Once again, it’s a case of the parable of the grasshopper and the ants cited earlier in this book.

Let your less farsighted friends be the grasshoppers. You be the wise ant looking ahead and preparing for a secure and worry-free future.

> **A bank is a place where they lend you an umbrella in fair weather and ask for it back when it begins to rain.**
>
> ***– Robert Frost***

95.

Save at Major Chain Stores

There are huge savings to be found at major retail and grocery chain stores. That's if you know how to take advantage.

Later in this book, I'll point you to several outstanding blogs and websites which are frequently updated and will furnish you with the latest money-saving tips.

However, there are some basics to cover here that will make an impact on your finances, especially when it comes to your supermarket expenditures.

The first fact to consider is that all grocery chains are not created equal.

I do the grocery shopping for our household, and my wife does the cooking.

We have six grocery chains operating in our city — and two more if you include the super Target and Walmart stores. Each, in my opinion, has its strengths and weaknesses.

However, there is one chain where I buy almost 90 percent of our total purchases. I'll shop at some of the others on occasion, especially when there's a good deal on a special item that isn't available where I regularly shop.

And while it's not my preference to cite names of businesses in this book, I would be derelict if I didn't tell you about my experiences shopping at a Kroger-owned chain, Fry's, which operates in Arizona.

I almost feel a sense of guilt shopping at Fry's, the savings are so incredible. On the first Wednesday of each month they give seniors a ten percent discount on all grocery items. On top of that, I'm always on the lookout for "club member" specials. When I see a special that's a product we regularly use, I stock up. I have the benefit of a substantial club discount plus the 10 percent senior discount.

But, it doesn't stop there. Often, I'll have with me a handful of manufacturer's coupons that I've bought online from an eBay seller at a bargain price. These add to my total savings.

And there's more. About once a month, Fry's sends me and other club members a personalized packet of Fry's store coupons that are selected and target-printed by a computer that has stored data about our individual purchasing habits.. These contain coupons good for discounts on items that we regularly buy.

Many are for Kroger brand products which I find are of high quality and comparable to nationally-advertised brands, but sell for about half the price.

Occasionally, Fry's offers a super discount on special items when you buy five or more of the same item. That's when I stock up big time.

By the time I get to the checkout, my net savings almost always amount to at least one-third off my total grocery bill. We're talking serious money here when a typical gross amount might be $180 and you pay only $120 at checkout.

There are additional benefits. I pay with a VISA credit card that returns two percent cash back on *all* purchases, no matter what. So, there's yet an additional discount on the grocery total.

And according to numerous survey articles that appear in the local newspaper, Fry's is typically among chains on record as having the lowest supermarket totals for identical or similar market baskets when compared to its competition.

There's yet one more bonus. Fry's also sells gasoline and for every dollar you spend on groceries, Fry's posts one point to your gasoline discount account. If you've spent let's say $200 during a particular month, then you have accumulated 200 points. And when you go to the pump, the computer will deduct 20 cents a gallon from your entire fill-up. For us, that's usually 40 cents a gallon for a twelve-gallon fill-up, representing an additional savings of $4.80.

I wish to declare here that no consideration has been paid me by either Fry's or the Kroger Corporation for mentioning or promoting their stores, and I have not consulted with or contacted them in connection with this book or chapter. I have reported this because it's just too good not to include.

> **Without frugality none can be rich, and with it very few would be poor.**
>
> ***– Samuel Johnson***

96.

Save on Gasoline

Because a substantial portion of many household budgets is spent on transportation, it is to your advantage to bring this cash-gobbling giant under control.

One way to accomplish this is to judiciously use the gasoline points that are awarded when you shop at a supermarket chain that also sells gasoline. Each chain has its own set of rules for using and accumulating points. You should familiarize yourself with the rules and then devise a strategy that will allow you to benefit the most.

Some chains have an expiration date for points while others are more generous. Also, most will limit you to the number of gallons for which you can receive discounts at any one fill-up. Often this number is around 30 gallons.

If you have two vehicles in your household, and let's say one is a passenger sedan with a gas tank holding 12 gallons and the other an SUV with a 20-gallon capacity, you will want to use your gasoline points to fill the SUV. You will realize your maximum savings if you fill up when your tank is close to empty.

And don't let your points expire. Keep track.

Some more obvious strategies for saving on gasoline include limiting your trips to purchase groceries, pharmaceuticals and sundry items. In other words, don't buy things one at a time unless they are perishable.

Another way to save is to limit your trips overall. A 20-minute drive to the shopping center will cost you in both gasoline and time off from productive endeavors if you add up the total time it takes you away from home or business.

I use the Internet to buy almost everything I need short of groceries and gasoline. Doing this has saved me hundreds of hours of valuable time. Shopping malls haven't seen me in ages. Why should I travel to a mall, contend with the hassle of crowds and then be told by a store clerk, "If you don't see it on the shelf, it means we don't have it." Brilliantly informative — *not*!

Usually, a little bit of searching on the Internet will bring me exactly the item I'm looking for and in a couple of extra moments provide me with a list of online merchants offering the item and their prices so that I can choose the best deal. Calculate how much gas and time are saved in just one of these transactions. This is time that you could otherwise use to build your business.

Next, we come to economy vehicles. This might not be the time for you to buy a new vehicle, but it might be wise to plan when to do so. Everything I've read and heard from owners, the Toyota Prius, a hybrid vehicle, is both the most frugal and reliable vehicle when it comes to gasoline use.

If you are putting on lots of mileage, a vehicle of this kind that gets you up to 50 miles per gallon of gas must be considered.

Should you require a pickup truck for your work or business, you should do a lot of research and talk to pickup truck owners regarding warranties, frequency of repair, etc. Some truck owners have complained bitterly to me about huge repair expenses that weren't covered by warranty. Shop with great care.

Last, it's important to mention a policy that some of my regular vendors were forced to implement when gas reached $4.00 a gallon.

One vendor imposed a flat $5.00 fuel surcharge which he added to each bill for service calls.

Another added a $10.00 trip charge if the customer lived more than 10 miles from his home base.

In short, it's vitally necessary to keep a tight handle on transportation costs or they can end up putting you and your business in the red.

97.

Super Used Book Source

While most of the information we seek can be found online, there are exceptions, especially if you are looking for details about a complex subject, one which would require a book on the subject rather than a few paragraphs as might be found online.

Instead of buying a new book, you can save money by first checking to see if it's available at your public library. But, if it's not, here's a tip.

Buy a used copy. My first stop is an online website, betterworldbooks.com. Why? First, because it's a charitable organization with all profits going to teaching literacy throughout the world.

betterworldbooks.com receives many of its books as donations from public libraries which have excess and need shelf space for new books.

This website identifies each book as either hardback or paperback, so you will know exactly what you're ordering.

Also, betterworldbooks.com ships for free. Yes, free! Their average price for a used book is about $4.00 and they note the condition of each book.

For myself, I really don't care much about the book's condition as long as it's readable. I don't buy books with leather covers to decorate my bookshelves or to impress my friends.

Other vendors of used books include abebooks.com which maintains the largest database of any bookseller anywhere and Amazon.com. There's also alibris.com. Check out those sellers, too.

98.

Never Pay Interest or Fees

Never pay interest or a fee for *anything,* if you can help it. You think I'm kidding?

If financial institutions had to rely on what I've spent on fees in the last fifty years, most would have gone out of business.

First, there are free checking accounts to be had if one takes the time to find them. They might not be available at the convenient bank branch located down the street from where you live, but someplace in America — remember, you can access any bank or credit union via the Internet — there are financial institutions waiting to open an account for you without monthly fees and no minimum balance to maintain. You just need to search.

Beware! Many banks charge as much as $15.00 a month to maintain a simple personal checking account and then on top of that some will make you pay extra if you want to talk to a teller or other human. You'll usually find the highest charges at the big name banks, those with a nationwide presence.

An example of a free checking account and its extra benefits and bonuses was a promotion I recently received in the mail for a Discover Bank Cash-Back Checking Account. There are no monthly fees, no minimum balance requirement, free standard checks, no-fee ATMs and much more. Whether this type of account will be available when you read this is uncertain. But the point is that free checking accounts do exist.

When it comes to credit card companies, also beware. If you're truly a money saver or have decided to become one, you will be shopping for a credit card that offers the highest cash back percentage on *all* purchases, not just on selected ones. The interest rate should be of no consequence because it only makes sense to use the card if you are going to pay the entire bill each month. If you begin carrying a balance, you defeat the entire purpose, which is to save money and stay out of debt. Instead, why not let the card issuer pay *you* for using their card? Paying in full each month also avoids late fees which can set you back even further.

There are also other late fees which you can avoid by paying on time. These include most utility bills, retail store charge account statements and mortgage payments. Be sure to pay all of these before the due date.

And if you can't afford to buy a certain item because you don't have the money to pay for it immediately, postpone your purchase. If it's a critical item that you can't live without, such as replacing a hot water heater, then postpone another less critical item and use that money to pay for the hot water heater.

If I find myself hit for a fee, which is almost never, it completely ruins my day. I often feel like a baseball pitcher who has served up a home run ball to a batter when his team was leading and he virtually had the game in his pocket.

Such fees are wasteful and unnecessary expenses and rank together with other unnecessary outlays, such as money spent on express shipping when the shipment could have been sent via ordinary channels were it ready on time.

Bringing expenses like these under control can make the difference between profit and loss for you and your business.

99.

Secondhand Savings

Whenever possible, buy secondhand for you, your home and your office.

It makes sense from several standpoints. First, you obviously will be paying less. And while that's important, so is the issue of quality.

Much of what is made today is low quality at best and shoddy at worst. Often, you can't find quality merchandise even if you're willing to pay more. It's just not out there.

Once, years ago, I was planning to stop at a couple of yard sales in my neighborhood in search of furniture for my house, which was bare at the time.

But, before departing, I phoned my Uncle Max in New York, who was considered the wise man of the family.

As we were wrapping up the conversation, Uncle Max asked what were my plans for the day. When I told him, he offered these words of advice: "My boy, buy only the best quality furniture. You cannot *afford* cheap furniture."

Lesson learned, Uncle Max. I still have some of the tables and chairs that I bought that day. They were in excellent condition and came out of an upscale house where a total renovation was in progress. And the price was fantastic. What a bargain!

Furniture, clothing and appliances are among items that you often can pick up secondhand and that prove to be of better quality than what is available new.

Back then, I bought a mixer that I had to recently toss out. Not because it wasn't still working well but because replacement blades for that model were no longer available.

We are still using a Maytag washer/dryer set that performs flawlessly. Price was $100 per unit, bought used 29 years ago. That's quality.

Obviously, electronic devices do not fit into this category because even when you buy new, the device can become obsolete within a year, and sometimes even within six months.

If you're embarrassed because your friends might find out that you are buying used merchandise, don't tell them. If they should find out, inform them that you're frugal and ask if that's a sin.

> **He is richest who is content with the least; for content is the wealth of nature.**
>
> **– *Socrates***

100.

Coupons Can Save Money

While coupons can save you money, learn to use them judiciously.

What is meant by that is that *all* coupons will not necessarily result in a net savings for you.

Take for example a jar of peanut butter. You have a coupon worth 50 cents or one dollar off a jar of brand name peanut butter. The brand name jar usually is priced at around $4.00, which means that you can save up to one dollar using a coupon.

However, if the grocery chain where you shop offers their own store-brand peanut butter for $2.20 and you find it be of quality equal with the brand-name peanut butter, then you'll end up paying about a dollar more if you use the coupon to buy the brand-name peanut butter.

You'll need to do your math and also compare the store-brand product with the popular brand and let your taste buds tell you if they are of equal quality and which tastes better to you.

I've already mentioned in a previous chapter how you can buy coupons in bulk from eBay sellers.

Some chain stores will limit the number of coupons you are allowed to tender for a single product such as a canned vegetable, coffee or a cleaning product while other chains will allow unlimited coupons.

Again, it only makes sense to use coupons when you can realize a net savings over the chain store's own brand, assuming that the chain's brand is equal in quality to the nationally-advertised brand.

You can also get coupons online. Problem is that many websites that boast printable coupons require you to sign up or register and then after you've done so you find that they don't have coupons for the products you're seeking even though they showed up on the Internet search.

If you are shopping online only, there are several websites that provide coupon codes to enter when making a purchase. Many will allow you to search or list their coupon codes in alphabetical order. Two of my favorites are www.retailmenot.com and www.couponcabin.com

Remember, there's a difference between paper coupons that you tender when reaching the checkout at your supermarket and coupon codes that you enter when checking out online. You will find more on this subject later in this book.

> **Annual income twenty pounds,**
> **annual expenditure nineteen six,**
> **result happiness.**
> **Annual income twenty pounds,**
> **annual expenditure twenty pound ought**
> **and six, result misery.**
>
> ***– Charles Dickens***

101.

Shop Thrift Stores

Many women friends of my wife and mine have told me they would be embarrassed (*mortified* was the word one woman used) if they were seen by one of their friends coming out of a thrift shop.

Well, I say if your survival depends on remaining solvent, let those who criticize you be the ones who should be mortified. You need to stretch your money and you can very often find great buys in a thrift shop.

Frequently, thrift shops will have a sale on all merchandise, most of which is already price-tagged extremely low.

In the larger thrift stores, most of which are operated by charities or religious organizations, you can find almost anything except food. These stores are a terrific place to buy books, DVDs and magazines, too.

And you'll find some of the best buys on furniture in thrift stores. Often good furniture pieces sell for a fraction of what you might pay retail for new furniture. You can also find these buys at yard sales or garage sales or advertised online.

However, you always need to carefully check out what you're buying and if appropriate ask about return policies.

And if you're really too embarrassed to shop at a local thrift store, consider driving to a nearby community where you likely won't be recognized.

102.

Hire Only the Best

It doesn't really cost any more to hire the best. And, when you do so, you will often end up saving money.

Why? Because when you hire a second- or third-string professional, you are getting what you pay for. And often that can be very expensive because you might later need to hire a first-stringer to fix errors and problems caused by the professional who worked cheaper.

This is no joke and I see it happening often.

Most top-of-the-line professionals, including doctors, lawyers and accountants, not only keep up to date on the latest changes and developments in their specialized fields, but also are fully familiar with the internal workings of various government offices that relate to their practice. For example, an attorney might suggest, "Let's wait until next week to file our papers because Mr. A. will be back from vacation and he isn't as tough on new applicants as Mr. B., who will be away on temporary assignment then."

I was fortunate once to consult a lawyer who kept abreast of real estate tax legislation to the extent that he received a daily report from Capitol Hill as to what a House committee was considering in connection with a measure to change laws governing the tax-free exchange of real property. He was in a position to advise me on a subject on that particular day when most other lawyers or accountants couldn't do so because they lacked that same information — information that would pass into their hands later, but too late for me.

Also, when you hire the best within a certain specialty, they often are accorded privileges that the average practitioner doesn't enjoy. This applies in medicine as well. Not long ago, I contacted a medical specialist while seeking information on behalf of a relative. In a half hour, the specialist phoned me back saying, "I just talked to one of the top experts in the country at Massachusetts General Hospital and he told me that as of this moment there have been no new advances in the treatment of this disorder."

You'll also find that in any community the best know the best. This is true in virtually all fields. It seems that the best tax lawyer can direct you to the best immigration lawyer and the best primary care physician can tell you who are the best surgeons.

There's a handyman in our city — let's call him Jack — and though technically speaking he doesn't fit into the classification of a professional, he charges only slightly more than other handymen. We use his services for almost everything and my wife always says, "If you hire Jack, you pay a little bit more, but you only have to pay him once. He does the job right the first time."

Overall, my rule is if the issue impacts on your health, your family or your finances, settle for no one but the best-qualified person in that field. It's not the time to bargain hunt.

> **A penny saved is a penny earned.**
>
> ***– Benjamin Franklin***

103.

Save Big with Free Shipping and More

If you do some of your shopping online, you likely already know that you can often get free shipping depending on the dollar amount of your purchase(s).

Free shipping can be a substantial money-saver if you play your cards right. And you can save much more than just the shipping costs.

For example, if you are shopping for a non-perishable product that you use or consume the year round and there's no concern about spoilage, you can combine a six-way savings.

Yes, you read that right. A *six-way* savings on a single purchase.

Let's say you are buying Product X and you have already scoured the Internet to find the lowest price and you've checked out the seller's reliability.

Nailing down the lowest price represents Savings Number One.

Next, determine how much you need to spend on a single shipment to qualify for free shipping. Since you're buying a non-perishable item, such as socks or paper or storage bins, etc., you can increase the size of your order to meet the free-shipping minimum. By meeting that requirement, you've achieved Savings Number Two.

Then, find out how many units of the product you need to additionally purchase to advance to the next volume or quantity price break. Perhaps, you'll qualify for the very lowest volume price if you buy eight or more units instead of the six units that you originally intended to buy. That's Savings Number Three.

Next, if you've landed on a website business that has no physical presence in your state, then you'll not be charged sales tax. That's Savings Number Four.

To take your fifth savings, you need to find a viable discount coupon code that you enter at checkout. This can often amount to five, ten or sometimes up to twenty percent.

We discussed this previously in Chapter 100, and there is more about online coupon codes later in this book.

Finally, are you ready for your sixth and final savings? Pay for your purchase online by using a cash-back credit card. Mine returns two percent on all purchases. There are no exceptions. All purchases are included.

There is your six-way savings. And you don't even need to leave your house! What's not to like?

> **Cannot people realize how large an income is thrift?**
>
> ***– Cicero***

104.

Computer Printer Savings

A lot of money is spent, much of it unnecessarily, replacing computer printer inkjet cartridges.

We have two older desktop computers which my wife and I keep busy throughout the day and evening. One is equipped with a ten-year-old black and white laser printer and the other with a new state-of-the-art inkjet printer.

I use the laser printer several times a day and often for printing out large files. I probably go through between 15 and 20 reams of paper per year. However, it's necessary to replace my toner cartridge no more than once or twice a year. That puts my toner usage cost somewhere between $25.00 and $50.00 annually.

My wife, whose printing volume is substantially lower than mine, must replace all of her color ink cartridges somewhere between two and three times a year at a cost of about $50.00 for each refill package.

But, here's the kicker. My wife has what the manufacturer boasts is an "economy" printer when it comes to ink usage *and* my wife selects "gray scale" for all black and white printing jobs that will be read only by us. That's what is called an economy setting. And as a further money saver, she uses the gray scale setting for printing almost all pages from the Internet, being aware that most are in color and require lots of color ink when they are printed.

If she wants to have some of her photos printed, she sends them via email to either Costco or Walgreen's which can do the job cheaper than we can do it at home, considering the cost of color ink.

If all of these cost-saving measures were not utilized and if all printing, including Internet color pages, were printed using the normal settings and if we printed our photos at home, we would see an inkjet cartridge replacement bill running into the hundreds of dollars per year. Who needs that?

Take heed. This is a significant savings and it's money you can put to better use elsewhere.

> **Economy is a savings bank into which men drop pennies and get dollars in return.**
>
> ***– Josh Billings***

105.

Utility Rates for Low-Income Users

Not everyone knows about this, but in most states public utilities including telephone, electric, natural gas, water and Internet service providers are required to offer special reduced rates for low-income customers.

Although several utilities are mentioned above, it's unlikely that in any state or community you will find *all* of these utilities offering such reduced rates.

Rather it might be one or two of those mentioned.

If you are currently unemployed, it's likely that you could qualify for such reduced rates. Especially if the requirement is based solely on current income.

Best is to get on the phone and check with each separate utility.

And if you follow the advice given in the next chapter, you won't just ask twice, you'll ask three times. You can't rely on what one person tells you over the phone. Especially, when it's important to you.

106.

Don't Ask Twice; Ask Three Times

Have you noticed that the quality of service is slipping and errors have become a way of life?

A case in point: Recently, I needed some equipment for my computer printer. I phoned the authorized local dealer only to be informed they were out of stock and that the item was no longer being made. A call to the manufacturer's warehouse, however, disclosed that the equipment was indeed still available, though in limited quantity. Three days later, the item was delivered to my mailbox.

Such similar experiences are an everyday occurrence in my life.

It was my wife's cousin who introduced us to the "Ask Three Times" rule. It pays off when asking directions, checking prices and in many other situations. You simply should not rely on the first answer you're given.

Receiving erroneous or incorrect information can prove costly to you. Go the extra mile and ask three times.

107.

Money-Saving Websites

There are literally hundreds of excellent money-saving websites which can help you reduce your expenses.

And take heart, reducing one's expenses does not necessarily require lowering one's standard of living.

That's why these money-saving techniques are so critical to your financial recovery. You can live well while spending less money.

These are four of the best money-saving websites:

www.tiphero.com

www.nerdwallet.com

www.livingonthecheap.com

www.clarkhoward.com

(Note: The Clark Howard website is also mentioned in Chapter 37 about Work at Home offers.)

The volume of useful information contained on these websites is nothing short of amazing. They will have links taking you to yet more websites where you'll find additional useful information, ideas and motivation.

However, I urge you not to get too caught up with the money-saving aspect as it can become addictive and consume too much valuable time that you could be devoting to building your business.

Instead, parcel out your time for investigating ways to save and instead put your prime time into increasing earnings. Whether it's serving your customers, promoting your business or working at a part-time or temporary job until your own business can support you, adding to your income must remain your top priority.

A key part of your new persona is to see yourself as a business person *first* and as a consumer second.

> **There are plenty of ways to get ahead. The first is so basic I'm almost embarrassed to say it: spend less than you earn.**
>
> ***– Paul Clitheroe***

108.

Rebuild Your Credit

If you've had a bankruptcy or your credit card issuer will no longer extend you credit, you might be facing a "no credit card" crisis. But, don't despair. There's a solution. Perhaps, more than one.

Because you'll need either a credit or debit card to function as a businessperson, you need to get busy on this.

There are basically two types of cards which are commonly issued to individuals who have bad credit ratings. One is the pre-paid debit card. The other is a credit-building card.

With both cards you'll need to make an advance deposit. Some card issuers require a deposit as low as $200.00.

There are several websites which rate these cards. Three are listed below. Visit these sites to obtain detailed information. You'll find that some of the card issuers charge no annual fee.

www.bestprepaiddebitcards.com/credit-building-cards/

www.bankrate.com/finance/banking/best-prepaid-debit- cards.aspx

www.nerdwallet.com/blog/bankingnerdwallets-best-prepaid-debit-cards/

The purpose of maintaining an excellent record once you receive one of these cards, especially the credit-building card, is to enable you to qualify for a card with improved benefits in the future.

However, I must emphasize here the point that I make throughout this book, and that is that a credit card or any other type of credit should only be used for immediate convenience.

Under no circumstances should you ever carry a balance. Pay your credit card statement balance in full every month — always.

A credit card is a necessity to take advantage of bargains on the Internet.

My advice: Use it to make a purchase, but only if you have funds to pay for it at the end of the month or when you receive your bill. If you don't have the money; don't buy it. You cannot afford to get into debt. You must remain debt free to prosper.

I have never maintained a balance and I have saved thousands of dollars in interest as a result. You can do the same.

109.

A "Must Read"

There is one publication whose issues I make it a point never to miss reading. It's *Bottom Line Personal*, a twice-monthly, 16-page newsletter.

I cite it because rarely have I come across an issue in which I don't find an item that will either save me money or time or help in maintaining good health.

There are many useful consumer publications in circulation, but in my opinion this one stands out as the most valuable to me.

Over the years, *Bottom Line Personal* has provided me with both health and consumer protection as well as business inspiration on a number of levels. I truly believe that as an entrepreneur this is one publication I can't do without.

The subscription cost is modest, but if you want to save money by not taking out a subscription, you will likely find it available at your public library.

Or you might interest a friend in subscribing and sharing the cost.

Every time I come across an item in *Bottom Line Personal* that I can put to use, I find myself remarking to my wife that the item in question just paid for a year's subscription.

110.

Save on Subscriptions

A natural follow-up to the previous chapter is to detail how you can save on both print and online subscriptions.

That mentioned in the previous chapter can save you perhaps $25 a year, but when you consider what you might need to spend to maintain a subscription to a daily local newspaper or to a national newspaper, it can easily run in the hundreds of dollars.

Instead, talk to a neighbor — neighbors are best because of proximity — and try to arrange it so that you subscribe to one publication and the neighbor to another. Minimum savings here: Anywhere from $150 to $250 a year.

With the price of annual subscriptions increasing every year, sharing makes good sense.

You can also save by negotiating or taking advantage of special subscription deals, especially when it comes to renewals.

I recently received a renewal notice for a business publication to which I subscribe. "Hurry!" the notice read. It offered a renewal for $49.95 for one year. I checked my own records and saw that last year I paid only $29.95 for a one-year renewal, so I decided to phone the call center which handles subscriptions for the publication in question.

My first question was to ask the agent if there were any two- or three-year renewals available. She said that she could offer me a two-year renewal for $50.00. Without skipping a beat, I provided her with my credit card number.

A personal finance magazine offered a two-year renewal for $30.00. The previous two-year renewal was $20.00. So, I phoned a magazine call center that renewed my subscription for three years at a cost of $30.00.

If the above tactic doesn't work in a particular case, you have another option to try. Wait them out. Publishers don't like to lose a loyal subscriber, and some will go to great lengths to keep you on their subscriber rolls. If you wait, and sometimes even allow your subscription to lapse, you'll continue to receive mailings urging you to "come back." Often, one of these will include a super deal. That's when you jump.

Sometimes, my wife will wait for a publisher to send her a holiday gift offer. Sign up for a gift subscription for a friend or relative at half price. Often, there's an option accompanying the offer, that being to extend your own subscription, also at half price. She almost always takes advantage of these, and now has one publication to which she subscribes that expires six years from now.

> **Beware of little expenses;**
> **a small leak will sink a great ship.**
>
> ***– Benjamin Franklin***

111.

Pay "Real People" First

When I look at my stack of bills, I always try to pay "real people" first. After that I pay bills that are generated by a computer.

Of course, I always strive to pay *all* bills before their due dates. Otherwise, it's not only costly having to pay penalties, but it affects one's credit rating.

The real people to whom I refer are the vendors, professionals, service people and others that I interface with on a personal level. Paying these folks promptly helps them to meet their obligations and makes you a good guy in their eyes.

Another way to look at this is that if you are able to pay one of your vendors upon receipt — even if it would be acceptable to him/her if you paid within ten days — such acts of consideration are certain to be appreciated.

Your paying on the day you receive the bill will be remembered because it is so unusual and will also buy you goodwill. And that's priceless.

In contrast, whether you pay a utility or a large corporation a couple of weeks prior to the due date or if you pay on or close to the due date a computer will record the payment, but no human will think better or worse of you for it.

When you perform a kindness for a real person, someone remembers.

112.

Patronize "Real People"

As a follow-up to the previous chapter, a similar line of thinking also applies to whom you choose to do business with.

Undeniably, there are times when you have no choice but to make your purchase at a big box store or insure your car with one of the nation's insurance giants.

However, there are other times when you have some options as to where to take your business.

For example, whenever possible, my wife and I will choose an independently-owned restaurant in preference to a chain-owned.

At the locally-owned eatery, the owner is usually on the premises and will often greet you when you enter. After a few visits, you'll have a sense of belonging. You'll know them and they will know you.

For me, chain-owned businesses seem cold and impersonal. It's rare that you will see the same employees there year after year. Your patronage means nothing to anyone connected with the business.

Think about this, too. The profits from independent businesses remain in the community. They aren't shipped to the headquarters offices of the chains, which might be in New York, Chicago or Los Angeles, if not abroad.

Other independent businesses that can serve you well are repair garages, yard good stores, book stores, banks, florists, bakeries and a wide range of service-oriented businesses.

When patronizing these independently-owned businesses, take time to introduce yourself to the owner or manager. Hand them one of your business cards. They may very well someday become *your* customer.

113.

Rent from Individuals

If you think this issue is small potatoes, think again. If you are going to be renting property, either residential or commercial, strike a deal with the individual owner of the property, not a corporation or a property management company.

First, there are many small investor landlords who, if they can secure a responsible tenant who will take good care of the property and pay the rent on time, will rarely increase the rent when the lease expires. Also, if the owner views you as a good prospective tenant (based on credit reports and a face-to-face meeting), you can negotiate a good deal for yourself.

In contrast, corporate-owned rental property generally offers no possibility for negotiation. Managers are handed their rules and policies from higher up and are most often bound by them.

Even worse, if you're living or working in a corporate-owned property, you can almost count on rent increases each time your lease comes up for renewal.

I have a relative living on the East Coast who has occupied the same apartment for more than 30 years. The complex is owned by a mega-corporation. Every year, her rent increases by five percent. No matter what! Good economy or recession.

If you are living anywhere except perhaps in New York, Boston or San Francisco, and you are renting from a private owner, you will likely have some leverage when it comes lease renewal time.

You can point out that you've been a model tenant, paid your rent on time and are an asset to the property. You can also point out that your salary hasn't increased in the last couple years and that you can't afford an increase. You add that you might have to move if there is an increase.

An individual landlord will give your situation some thought while the on-site manager for a corporation most often doesn't have such discretion. You might as well be talking to a computer.

In many instances, rental policy is set by the headquarters office of a Real Estate Investment Trust, otherwise known as REIT. Some REITs own and manage apartment complexes numbering hundreds of units in more than a dozen cities.

Beyond all that, there is something so impersonal about residing in a corporate-owned house or apartment. There is often rapid turnover of management, so it's unlikely that after a couple years anyone in management would be around to know what a good tenant you are or for that matter, care.

An individual owner is dependent on you to both take good care of his property as well as provide him/her with income. This owner will usually be quite aware of who you are and what kind of a tenant you are. And very often, he/she will want to please you so that you will stay.

Further, I speak from experience on both ends.

> **The most substantial people are the most frugal, and make the least show, and live at the least expense.**
>
> ***– Francis Moore***

114.

Vacation Without Hotels, Resorts or Tents

Ever heard of VRBO?

VRBO is an acronym for Vacation Rentals By Owner. It's exactly what the name implies.

Next time you vacation, try renting a free-standing vacation rental house or condo instead of a hotel or motel room. It's often more economical and more comfortable, too. No sitting on the edge of the bed to watch TV.

Vacation homes are an especially wise choice if you are vacationing as a family. You won't need to book additional rooms; you'll have a real kitchen and perhaps a garage and laundry.

You get a place to park your car, privacy, nobody walking the floors above you after midnight, no TV blaring from the next room, etc. Also, you won't need to run out for breakfast or other meals. It's a home away from home. And you'll be staying in a residential neighborhood — not by the noisy freeway access ramp.

We've been staying in vacation rental houses or flats for the last twenty years. You can book online at VRBO as well as on some smaller websites or you can search further using Google or craigslist.org.

I recommend using VRBO because it's well-organized and you can read reviews of most properties.

I also use TripAdvisor.com for ratings on everything else in whatever location we're visiting, including restaurants, attractions, etc.

Another source for finding good deals is using Google to take you to the Chamber of Commerce or tourist bureau websites for the particular town or area you intend to visit. Often these carry links to vacation rentals.

Vacation rentals are great for relaxing, enjoying and saving money at your travel destination. Typically, these rent by the week or month. In popular resort areas, you might find some that rent by the night or weekend.

And here's an added tip: Once you've selected your candidate for the vacation rental you want, try to ask someone you know or a friend of someone you know who lives in that town to do an onsite inspection.

It's not as difficult as you might think to arrange this. You've heard of "six degrees of separation." If you need someone to inspect a vacation rental for you in a vacation community, you compose an email message asking if anyone knows someone who lives in that community or has a summer place there, etc.

You then send the message to all your friends and relatives in your email address book. It will be the rare occasion that there isn't someone who knows someone who is familiar with that particular community.

And it's not essential that the person familiar with that community is physically present in that community at the time of your contact. If you are introduced via phone to that individual, you can ask if they know anyone who is living there now. Get a name and phone number and contact the persons saying that John or Jean gave you their name. And be sure to send a thank-you note.

I must confess that we've learned about the need to do this from life experience. Photos that you see on the Internet don't always tell the whole story. For example, strange odors can't be detected in the photos that you see on the website.

115.

When to Make a Loan? Never. And Here's Why

You don't need to go back to Polonius in Shakespeare's *Hamlet* to heed this advice: "Neither a borrower or a lender be."

Making loans to friends or relatives so often ends badly. Such casual loans are often not repaid or not repaid on schedule and end with the loss of a friendship or hard feelings within the family.

If a friend or relative is financially hurting and you want to help, you are far better off making an offering of cash to the person. If the circumstances are such that the recipient's pride needs to be salvaged, you can add, "Pay me back when you can."

If you find yourself squeezed between relatives' expectations and practicalities and you're really not feeling good about extending yourself to someone whom you perceive to be a "net taker," you might explain that business has been slow or you've had to make some major repairs and that there's not much left in the checking account. Adding: "But look, if a couple of hundred dollars would help out, I can give you that."

This shows the relatives that you care, but it doesn't put you in a position where you must risk your own financial future. And if you never get paid back, the recipient will be too embarrassed to come asking again.

116.

Recreation on the Cheap

When money is scarce and discretionary spending has become virtually non-existent, don't whine. There's lots you can do for recreation and enjoyment at a cost so reasonable that you often can fund it with the loose change in your pocket.

First, consider the great outdoors. There are few locations in the U.S. where you won't find either a state or national park or forest nearby. Many are free and those charging admission are usually quite affordable, with the fee covering everyone riding in one vehicle.

If there are senior relatives in the family, their Golden Eagle Passport will admit the car free to any national park and most other federally-operated facilities. Some of the older-issued Golden Eagle passports even include free camping.

Day hikes provide fun and exercise for the entire family. You can pack a lunch and avoid the cost of eating out.

In certain states, such as California, there are so many public hiking areas that you might not be able to visit all of them during a lifetime.

For indoor entertainment, consider Netflix streaming. You and the family can choose from thousands of movies and play an *unlimited* number. All are available around the clock. Monthly cost as of this writing is $10.00. More about Netflix in Chapter 149.

And rather than order pizzas delivered, consider preparing your own popcorn. Not the microwave stuff, but the real thing. My wife makes it using peanut oil and special finely-ground popcorn salt.

117.

"Retired" — the Magic Word

Even before I left newspaper work to go into business for myself, I dreaded filling out applications for credit. Something as simple as requesting service from a utility company or moving into an apartment brought unending questions: "Where are you employed? For how long?" And it went on.

After I became self-employed, it got even worse. Now the questions were, "You don't have a job? Well, what do you do?" When I answered that I was self-employed, I was then asked to submit copies of my tax returns for the previous five years. And the tax returns had to show that I had sufficient income from my business during that period. Neat trick, if you just left your employment a few months earlier.

My solution to these Catch-22 barriers? I said "thank you" to the representative with whom I was speaking, then hung up the phone and immediately called the same number until I got a different representative.

When it came to the employment question, I answered "retired." I figured since I had retired from my newspaper job, it was a legitimate answer. Never mind that I was only 47 years old at the time.

Within minutes, the application was completed and I was instantly approved.

That was more than thirty years ago. Since then, I have answered "retired" each and every time with identical results. To date, no one has ever asked me from where I'm retired or how long or anything else.

"Retired" is truly a magic word.

118.

Cash-Back Credit Cards

There's a huge savings to be realized by using cash-back credit cards *if* you are able to exercise financial discipline. That means charging to your credit card *only* that amount — and no more — that you know you can pay in full when you receive your monthly bill.

At the time of this writing, for example, Capital One Bank offers a Spark Business VISA credit card which returns two percent cash-back on *all* purchases. No exceptions. No gimmicks. Just a flat two percent which is credited to your account.

Some of the bank's other VISA card products return a lesser cash-back percentage, so you must strive to get the Spark Business VISA specifically.

A retired friend, who we will call Mr. Jones, owns a rental condo together with his wife. They both manage the property. When Mr. Jones applied for the VISA card, he listed his business as Jones Management. He got the Business VISA and pays his bill in full each month.

He charges everything he can to that VISA card, including his telecommunications bills, auto and other insurances, etc. Basically, he reviews his fixed monthly expenses and queries each and every provider asking if they will automatically charge their monthly fees to his VISA account. Some do and some don't. And a few will charge a fee to do so. Those he rejects.

He figures his average monthly VISA bill ranges between $3,000 and $4,000 a month, bringing his annual cash-back awards to a range between $800 and $1,000 a year. Certainly nothing to sneeze at. And it's all tax free.

At the moment, there are not many credit card issuers who are paying two percent on cash-back cards. A couple of others that you can check out are Charles Schwab and Fidelity.

Also, you can try an Internet search as there are always new credit card products, including cash-back cards, being introduced.

> **Rich people stay rich by living like they're broke. Broke people stay broke by living like they're rich.**
>
> ***– Unknown***

119.

Take a Social Worker to Lunch

If at all possible, make friends with a social worker. He or she might be employed at a medical facility or by a government agency. You can arrange an introduction by putting out the word among your friends and acquaintances.

You will likely have questions related to your own medical concerns or perhaps you have aged parents who require services or are considering moving to a retirement or assisted living facility.

To be able to ask your questions and not be interrupted by phone calls and other workers, it would be to your benefit to invite the social worker to lunch, and be straightforward about needing to ask him/her questions related to health care, and of course, citing the name of the friend or acquaintance who referred you.

A sharp social worker will be in a position to advise you as to which facilities to consider and which to avoid. Also, if you have an aged parent who will require assistance from Medicaid — there exist few facilities nowadays where the cost is below $5,000 monthly — they will be able to walk you through the many bureaucratic steps needed to qualify for such programs.

There's a lot of misinformation being circulated, most of it unintentionally, but nevertheless frustrating if you find yourself spending a large amount of time, only to discover that you're on the wrong track.

A well-informed social worker can assist you in avoiding such pitfalls.

120.

Buying at Costco or Sam's Club

As many of you already know, shopping at one of these big box stores isn't the same as buying items for dinner at your neighborhood supermarket.

Yes, of course, prices are lower, but you must often buy in large sizes or quantities plus there's an annual membership fee. Also, most don't redeem manufacturers' coupons or accept all credit cards.

For instance, if you are going to shop at Costco you will either need to bring cash or pay with a VISA card. Formerly, an American Express card was the only credit card accepted, but that was to change in June, 2016.

If you are a single person, the lower prices may not be worth the membership fee for you to shop at one of these stores.

However, whether you're single or a member of a large family, there are huge annual savings which can benefit you if you are a regular consumer of certain over-the-counter products, daily supplements and pharmacy items, including prescriptions.

I know from my own experience that Costco, like Walgreen's, offers certain popular over-the-counter products that are often placed in stock alongside the brand name product and often at half the price. Customers can easily compare ingredients and often find that the ingredients are identical to that of the brand name product.

Buying a year's supply of one or more of these products can easily save the buyer several hundred dollars.

For couples, Costco annual membership begins to make more financial sense and for families of four or more you would be missing the boat if you didn't take full advantage of a membership.

For those facing hard times, one can stretch the budget for meals by buying perfectly healthy foods in large packages suitable for large families.

And if you have to pay for your prescriptions out of pocket, it's worthwhile to compare prices with the big box store pharmacies. Costco also offers its members — those who are eligible — a free membership in the Costco Prescription Club where a modest discount is applied to most orders. You can also enroll your dog or cat.

Also, most of these stores sell gasoline at reduced prices for members.

If you're in business, you can often find needed supplies cheaper, but it's still best to comparison shop via the Internet and check local wholesale suppliers.

Bottom line: Visit these stores with a friend or friends who are members and calculate whether it pays for you to take out a membership.

> **Wealth consists not in having great possessions, but in having few wants.**
>
> ***– Epicurus***

121.

How to Find Promo Codes

If you are buying any product on the Internet, be sure to first check if there's a promotion code for the vendor who is offering the item.

In an earlier chapter, we covered coupons in general and mentioned websites such as CouponCabin.com and retailmenot.com as good sources for both coupons and promo codes.

I still recommend going to these two sources first before trying other approaches. Your chances of success using these two websites are far better than those that follow here.

However, another way to track down promo codes (which can only be used for online purchases — not for in-store purchases) is to use a search engine such as Google.

This is how it's done. You find an exceptionally good buy on a pair of shoes at XYZshoes.com. Before you place your order, you minimize the page which shows the shoes you want. Then, bring up your Google search page.

In the search box, you enter XYZshoes and the words "promo code."

You'll usually find that a sizeable number of listings appear on your monitor screen. However, be alert. You'll find that only a few of the promo codes shown are usable.

Don't bother to click on those that take you to the merchant's home page. There will seldom be a promo code waiting for you.

Also disregard the listings that take you to a coupon website. As we already noted earlier, most of these sites will ask you for your information and send you lots of emails and promos, but you will seldom be able to access a usable promo code you want.

When you finally discover a site that offers real promo codes without diversions, you will often see that the site lists several promo codes for a particular merchant. It might also list the percent of individuals reporting success using a particular code. Some might have expired.

In addition to the codes you have already written down, include any different codes that you've gleaned from your Google search.

Write down only those codes that report a reasonable success rate. Some might not apply to your purchase so look for only those that can save you money today.

When you've written them all down, bring the XYZshoes page back up on your screen and proceed to the checkout.

At every checkout, there will be a place to enter a promo code. With your list in hand, try the most successful ones first. The merchant's software will reject those that aren't current or applicable and will inform you.

Sometimes a promo code will get you free shipping or a ten percent discount.

My own success rate with this process is around 25 percent, but as I often tell my wife, it's better than a kick in the pants.

Good luck!

122.

Cutting Utility Costs

Gas, oil and electricity to operate your heating and cooling systems are undoubtedly the major utility costs in every household.

And while it doesn't take a rocket scientist to figure out that your thermostat setting is a critical factor contributing to that cost, there exist other avenues for saving money on your bills.

My favorite money-saver has been shutting off heating or cooling to rooms that I don't use or use only during certain seasons.

Let's say that you are living alone in a three-bedroom house and you operate a home-based business. If you set up your home office where the sun will shine in you will get free passive solar heat for several hours most days. Also some of that heat will stay and slowly dissipate toward the evening. If you have an electric heater or other free-standing heating device working in that small office, it will keep you toasty warm if you keep the door closed and have good insulation. Double-paned windows or storm windows and doors will help further to keep costs down.

What about the remaining part of the house — the 90 percent or so that you aren't keeping toasty warm? You can afford to set the central heating thermostat at a low temperature, perhaps just enough to make sure no pipes freeze and that you can access other rooms such as the bathroom without needing to wear a parka.

During hot summers, you can set up a similar program. There are individual room air-conditioners available which can be installed in a wall and operate economically. If you have one of these in your home office, you can keep the rest of the house set at a much warmer temperature.

Of course, if you are part of a larger family, this won't work and you will need to devise a plan specifically geared to the health and comfort of all in your household.

And don't forget ceiling fans and portable fans. Although fans don't have any effect on the actual room temperature, it is reported that your body can feel at least two degrees cooler as a result of a fan operating nearby.

Also, did you know that most utility companies offer free analyses of your home utility usage along with recommendations for reducing costs? Take advantage of that expertise.

Many utility companies also offer reduced rates for electricity usage if you operate appliances such as washer/dryers, ovens, etc. during off-peak hours.

Finally, switching from incandescent light bulbs to either compact fluorescent or LED bulbs can result in substantial savings.

There are more detailed energy-saving tips available on the various money-saving websites on the Internet.

> **Whatever your income, always live below your means.**
>
> ***– Thomas J. Stanley***

123.

Spend Less, Eat Healthier

Believe it or not, there are benefits connected with reducing your spending and saving money. One of those can be an improvement in your health if you eliminate such items as steaks, liquor, junk foods and other pricey and unhealthy items from your shopping list.

Dr. Dean Ornish's Program for Reversing Heart Disease is a book you need to read, no matter your age. It contains advice, diets and other information for maintaining good heart health and overall body health. You can buy a used copy cheap from betterworldbooks.com or other used book websites.

If you're up to making changes in your life that will improve your health, this presents yet another opportunity. It costs much less to eat healthy because most of the recommended foods are fresh fruits and vegetables.

Example: Items such as yams and broccoli are often priced at 99 cents a pound where we shop. A good steak is often priced at between $8.99 and $12.99 a pound. If you're in your forties or beyond, Dean Ornish's book along with your doctor's advice, can help you toward a better life. However, since we're not in the practice of medicine, as the saying goes, first "Ask your doctor."

124.

Retention Specialist — What's That?

If you're seeking to lower your subscription rate to a publication or hold off an announced increase to your TV cable service, it's always more effective to immediately tell the representative answering your call that you wish to *cancel* your subscription. That's the magic word, *cancel.*

Most often, when you say that word you will be immediately connected to a retention specialist or "terrier" as they are sometimes called.

That's because their job is to save your account. They will try to persuade you to remain a customer and they will do everything possible to keep your account. Knowing this gives you an edge.

You'll find them working in diverse industries and service businesses including telecommunications, finance, insurance, health care and many others.

The retention specialist has discretion to make adjustments to your contract or offer you bonuses for renewal, etc., whereas the initial representative with whom you spoke first usually does not.

Although you will have mentioned that you wish to cancel, you are under no obligation to follow through.

See what concessions you can get from the retention specialist. Remember, you have no obligation to make a decision on the spot. You can say that you want to think it over or discuss it with your spouse or partner.

Sometimes, it pays to phone again the next day and try another retention specialist to see if you can negotiate a better deal.

A friend who is very adept at gaining concessions tells me that he is always quite humble when he talks with these folks and makes utterances such as, "I would like to accept your offer, but right now my reduced income just won't allow it." Or something similar. Put it into language that feels comfortable for you.

It is a rare day when you won't get some concession, no matter how small, from a retention specialist.

> **Save a part of your income and begin now, for the man with a surplus controls circumstances and the man without a surplus is controlled by circumstances.**
>
> ***– Henry H. Buckley***

125.

Tax Strategies

Hopefully, within a year or two of reading this, you will have reached a point in your economic recovery where you will be eager to get some tax relief. Not only from federal income taxes, but from self-employment tax, state income tax and a variety of other federal, state and local taxes.

Rather than approach this issue piecemeal by consulting friends, tax preparers and searching the Internet, it would be smart to begin by engaging the services of an experienced Certified Public Accountant (CPA). The more experienced he/she might be, the more likely you are to have someone that knows the answers to important questions. When I seek the services of a professional, whether it be a doctor, dentist, lawyer, etc., I always like to see some gray hair.

For me, some gray hair means "old enough to have had some experience." I like that.

But, that's only the half of it. The other half is finding a CPA who will voluntarily advise you when he or she comes across something that they think can benefit you taxwise.

There are many CPAs working in the field who are highly competent, will prepare your tax returns flawlessly, but will never call to your attention any tax strategies that will reduce your tax liability — unless you specifically ask.

Since you'll be paying around the same price for their service, why not choose a CPA who already has a track record for voluntarily calling to their client's attention any and all opportunities for reducing their taxes and allowing the client then to decide, "Is this something I want to do?"

When you interview prospective accountants, don't hesitate to ask directly, "Do you call clients' attention to tax-saving strategies, even if they haven't specifically asked a question about that issue?"

If you don't receive an answer that satisfies you, keep searching.

Do not underestimate the importance of the tax issue. I know many people who insist on doing their own tax returns believing they will save money by avoiding paying an accountant's fee. Wrong decision. They miss out on having benefit of the advice of an expert — one who can advise them on how to pay no more than is absolutely necessary in taxes and government fees.

In addition to having my tax returns prepared by a CPA, I have been subscribing for years to tax newsletters. If I come across an item that might apply to my own situation, I flag it and follow up with a call or email to my CPA asking if this new item is something that might apply to me and whether I can use it to reduce my tax bill.

Until not long ago, there were several tax newsletters published, but in recent years, I found only one that satisfies my needs and that is The Kiplinger Tax Letter. Try shopping around for the lowest subscription price.

You could also go 50-50 on the subscription fee with a friend, cut your cost and both of you benefit.

126.

Home Made Gifts

Remember when a nice birthday gift could be purchased with a $20 bill?

Now, a suitable gift costs between $35 and $50. Most hard-cover books run around $30.

If you have been laid off from your job, expenses for gifts can wreck your budget, especially if you have a large family or circle of friends. Yet you don't want to disregard an in-law's or cousin's birthday or anniversary, etc.

So what can you do?

Think home made gifts! For several years, my wife and a friend have teamed up to make jam and marmalade for holiday gifts. They make apricot jam from extra-ripe dried slab apricots purchased from a California orchard and the marmalade from tart Seville oranges from a tree in the friend's back yard. Both are delicious.

These two items have become such a hit with our friends and relatives, that we receive specific requests asking that we forego any store-bought gifts in favor of the jars of jam and marmalade.

The two also have other *applications* if I may for a moment invoke cyber jargon. A few weeks ago, I ran into a brick wall attempting to make an appointment with a medical professional. The staffers who make the appointments seemed unsympathetic and insensitive to my needs, which prompted me to ask to speak to a supervisor. I was soon connected and told the supervisor of the difficulties I had encountered.

The supervisor heard my story and subsequently found a way to work me into the schedule without waiting three months for an appointment. I was very grateful.

The next day, I stopped by the front desk at the medical facility carrying a small gift bag. Inside was a jar of the home made apricot jam nicely wrapped in white tissue paper along with a raffia ribbon and a thank-you card. The supervisor was delighted as well as surprised and I now have established some good will in that office.

If you are too busy to make home made gifts or lack the skills, as an alternative you can visit www.etsy.com and shop from among thousands of handmade gifts.

Remember, when you save like this, it really adds up.

True economy consists in always making the income exceed the outgo.

– P. T. Barnum

127.

This Saves Time and Money

Can you recall a day when you haven't been put on hold at least once?

One of the best investments I ever made was when I bought my first telephone headset. Today, I wouldn't be without one. A headset frees both hands so that I can write, leaf through catalogs or use the computer while on hold.

Using a headset also is more comfortable than holding the handset to your ear for long periods.

I never place a call from home unless I'm at my desk where I have my headset. If I'm put on hold, I can work on the computer, pay some bills or simply read. I would estimate that the headset enables me to make productive use of not less than a half-hour a week of otherwise dead time.

This can mean money in your pocket and a reduction in frustration of being kept on hold and watching your productive time being wasted.

> **The bitterness of poor quality remains long after the sweetness of low price is forgotten.**
>
> ***– Thomas J. Stanley***

128.

Money Down the Drain

When I lived in California, a friend told me that his annual expense for shampoo was $1.00 a year, and that he shampooed in the shower every day.

Needless to say, I was skeptical about his claim, but decided to play along. After all, I was spending $5.00 to $6.00 for a modest-sized squeeze bottle of shampoo which lasted perhaps a month. It was money going down the drain.

It turned out that my friend's secret was the local beauty supply shop which catered to the professional salon trade but also allowed sales to retail customers, in this case — me.

As recommended by my friend, I asked for a gallon of shampoo concentrate. I can't recall the name of the brand as it's been quite some time, but I remember that the cost of the gallon of concentrate was $16.00. Also, per my friend's instructions, I bought a couple of empty one-pint clear plastic squeeze bottles, and when I got home I thoroughly rinsed an empty one-gallon plastic milk container.

Then, I followed the instructions on the container, mixing a small amount of the concentrate with ordinary tap water. Next, I poured the mixture into the empty one-gallon milk container, then gently shook it.

I filled both squeeze bottles with my diluted shampoo concentrate from the mix in the container and set one of the squeeze bottles in the shower caddy.

After an entire year of shampooing in the shower daily, I noticed that the level of liquid in the concentrate container had scarcely dropped, perhaps less than an inch.

It turned out that the concentrate was enough to provide daily shampooing for one person for a period of sixteen years. Net cost: $1.00 per year.

I recently checked online and found that hair shampoo concentrate when bought by the gallon sells for between $17.00 and $50.00 a gallon depending on quality.

In all honesty, I must say that while the shampoo I used over those sixteen years was satisfactory in keeping my hair and scalp clean, it was no more than a basic cleansing agent. It contained no emollients, conditioners or extras of any kind. In a word, it was good basic shampoo.

I'm older now and require a bit more hair care than I did in my youth. So, I'm not doing the dollar-a-year number any more.

But, the opportunity to save still exists. Shop carefully, ask a lot of questions and search for information about the product online. Know what you are buying.

> **The borrower is servant to the lender.**
>
> ***– The Bible***

129.

Cutting the Cord

Most Americans are now familiar with the term "cutting the cord." For the benefit for those who aren't, it means discontinuing your cable or satellite TV service.

Why? First, because monthly subscription rates have increased at about twice the rate of inflation, but average family incomes have decreased. In other words it's getting pretty darn expensive.

Second reason, cable and satellite providers require you to accept a fixed menu, sometimes with as many as 200 channels. The upshot is that you are paying for channels that you don't watch. You might only regularly be watching one of half a dozen channels. However, if you would like to drop the 195 channels which you *don't* normally watch and pay for only those that you *do* watch, good luck. Your cable or satellite provider won't allow you to do that. It's all or nothing. Sorry.

It's not publicized, but the reason they won't allow you to pay for your desired channels a la carte is because your provider must pay the owners of each cable channel individually per subscriber. So, if your package includes let's say ESPN, the provider must pay ESPN a per subscriber fee of around $4.00 per month. That's a figure that's appeared in some news reports on the subject. However, the actual figure might be a bit more or less depending on current conditions. The reason for the high figure is that it costs ESPN thousands of dollars to televise a live sports event and those costs must be passed on to the consumer.

At the same time, the owner of a channel that provides only old movies 24/7 might charge your provider a fee of only ten cents a month per subscriber because his/her costs are substantially less.

So, if you were allowed to opt out of paying for ESPN and pay only, let's say, for some old movie channels, the satellite or cable operator's remaining subscribers — those who are sports fans — would be stuck with having to pay yet higher fees for their sports channels which might prove to be prohibitive. That being because the cost of televising a sports events is a fixed cost, and if you divide that cost among fewer subscribers you can easily figure what might be the net cost to each of the remaining sports subscribers.

Because I and millions of subscribers can't opt out of these pricey channels and don't wish to continue paying almost $100 a month for 200 channels of which we watch only about a half-dozen, we decided to cut the cord. And I have to tell you it felt great.

How families cope after cutting the cord varies. Some are content to simply go without any televised entertainment other than their free local over-the-air TV channels. Others will supplement with Netflix, Amazon, Hulu and a host of other video offerings.

If you are thinking of *cutting the cord*, enter those words in your Google search engine and read what others have to say. This is not a one-choice issue and there exist many options and alternatives. But you must consider it if you're really serious about reducing your personal expenses.

Do fully familiarize yourself with all of the ramifications of giving up cable or satellite reception before making a final move.

130.

Moonlighters

How often do you find yourself paying $75.00 an hour plus a hefty trip charge or minimum service charge to have a repair made in your home?

Whether the bill is from a plumber or a computer expert or garage door technician, such amounts seem high, especially for someone who isn't earning $75.00 an hour himself or herself.

There is another option for such repairs.

Before you call a repair service business listed online or advertised in the Yellow Pages, consider this.

Over the years, I've found skilled trades people who perform work at night and on weekends outside of their full-time jobs. For them, it's an opportunity to earn extra money, and most often they have received approval from their boss to moonlight as long as they are not taking customers away from the company that employs them.

Sometimes it can be a man who does electrical repair whose full-time job is working as a building inspector for the city or a woman who maintains information technology equipment for a large corporation and moonlights by solving home computer problems for her friends and neighbors.

When I was preparing to cut the cord on my TV satellite provider and switch to a combination of local TV, Internet video and Netflix streaming, I contacted a company which had been recommended for the work. They quoted me a fee of $100 an hour.

Since the point of eliminating my cable service was to *save* money, a $100-an-hour fee for someone to do the job didn't seem to make much sense.

So, I asked among my friends and located an experienced technician who performed unrelated work at his daytime job but was highly knowledgeable in the area of Internet protocol. He performed all the work needed at the more reasonable rate of $30 an hour.

> **Frugality, I've learned has its own cost, one that sometimes lasts forever.**
>
> ***– Nicholas Sparks***

131.

High-Rent Areas

Many towns and cities have one or more of what I call a "high-rent area."

You know what I mean — upscale, catering to the affluent. Mind you, I have nothing against these areas or the merchants and restaurateurs who lease their space. It's just that I can't afford them. And neither can you.

Often, I find that patronizing a store in a high-rent area that sells a product I want would result in my paying a substantial upcharge for the privilege of spending my money in a trendy neighborhood.

I understand that the lessee must pay a higher rent for his/her space than if the business were located elsewhere in town, but aren't there other areas I could choose to shop in?

I know my city fairly well and if I'm shopping for a product or a service I can usually tell from the address whether the price will be upped because of high rent.

This rule of thumb also usually applies to prices for gasoline, professional services, groceries, etc.

A few years ago, I drove to a carriage-trade food store in one of the high-rent areas in search of a hard-to-find product which it turned out they had in stock. As I walked through the aisles, I noticed the price of many standard packaged foods and observed that the prices were about 20 percent above what I would expect to pay at a large chain supermarket.

In the checkout line, the woman ahead of me, a Gucci bag on her shoulder, unloaded her groceries onto the conveyor belt. She had bought what appeared to be a full week's supply of groceries, and I was certain that during her shopping trip she had never once felt the need to look at the prices. Such was my impression. My point is that if you're reading this book, it's highly likely that you can't afford to go shopping without considering in what part of town you will shop and what prices you are prepared to pay.

> **The consumption society has made us feel that happiness lies in having things, and has failed to teach us the happiness of not having things.**
>
> ***– Elise Boulding***

132.

Free Directory Assistance

Why pay to look up a phone number? Years ago, this information was free. Phone companies now charge $1.50 or more to look up a single number for you. But, you can do something about it. All you need is a computer and you can look them up yourself for free.

Several websites offer free telephone directory information. They include:

www.exphonebook.com

www.anywho.com

www.411.com

www.switchboard.com

There are others, and similar new websites come online frequently.

On some of those websites you'll need to register first or navigate your way through to the white pages or yellow pages, depending on your needs.

It may take a bit of searching to find a free website that's user-friendly. However, once you've found the one that's right for you, add it to your list of "favorites" or "bookmarks." You'll find yourself saving money immediately.

My wife and I look up phone numbers at least twice a week. That represents a minimum savings of $300 per year. Not exactly small change.

There are also free websites for looking up phone numbers in Canada and other countries and some that enable you to do a reverse phone number search.

A number of these free websites also offer complete background checks, but for a fee.

Be careful to watch for these, especially if you are only seeking a free phone number lookup.

Some of the background checks include an extensive search of all public records, including criminal records, evictions and other legal data.

If you are without a computer or smartphone, but have telephone access, you can get free phone directory service by dialing toll-free 1-800-FREE411 [1-800-373-3411] from any phone in the United States.

You will need to listen to a sponsored advertising message before making your request.

The service is provided entirely by computer. There are no human operators. It's all done through voice-recognition, so you must speak clearly.

> **Thrift comes too late when you find it at the bottom of your purse.**
>
> ***– Seneca***

133.

How We Beat the Telemarketers

Hardly anything is more annoying than being interrupted by a telephone solicitor during dinner or while you're trying to work. My wife and I used to receive two or three telemarketer calls every evening. At the time, we didn't have an effective response except to say we weren't interested. That only brought out the telemarketer's "overcoming obstacles" script.

Since time is money, we needed to come up with a way to screen out these telemarketers and we've now developed an almost-foolproof strategy.

It's made possible by using a large or jumbo display caller identification (Caller ID) device that's considerably larger than the one on your phone or console. Its readout is large enough that it can be viewed from across a room.

Such units are approximately 2 to 3 inches in height and 8 to 10 inches in width. Most are available for purchase online.

Although the federal government adopted a DO NOT CALL law several years ago, it obviously has not been observed by telemarketers. We now receive at least twice as many telemarketer and robot calls than we did before DO NOT CALL.

It's become apparent that the telemarketers are aware that enforcement of DO NOT CALL lacks teeth and that their chances of being prosecuted for violation are extremely remote. I have not read or heard of a prosecution anywhere and have no knowledge or information about the size of the government's enforcement apparatus for this purpose. I suspect that it is minuscule.

And I want to emphasize that for many, telemarketer calls are more than a minor nuisance. They rob you of valuable time in your day.

We receive not less than three or four of these calls every day. Rain or shine.

And because certain categories of callers are exempt from the law, you'll get nowhere by relying on DO NOT CALL to curtail these unwanted calls.

Whether the telemarketer's call is exempted or not, we don't care. We screen out any incoming call that we don't recognize.

The telemarketers use all kind of tricks, such as it will appear in the caller ID readout, *Card Center* or *Electric Company*, wanting you to believe that your credit card issuer or local power company is attempting to reach you via phone.

Also, any call where the readout says identification is *Unavailable* is a reason not to pick up.

Usually, we don't need to get up out of our chairs if we're working at home to spot a telemarketer call. We've sharpened our skills at identifying them to the point where perhaps one in a hundred will get through.

If that happens and we pick up, as soon as we get the drift that it's a telemarketer, we simply say politely, "I'm sorry, but we don't accept solicitation calls. Thank you." And we immediately hang up.

Our telephone answering machine is connected to our primary residence phone. Rarely will a telemarketer leave a message unless it's a robot call. In case we're ever in doubt after rejecting a call, we can look at the answering machine and if we see that no message was left, we can be all but certain that the call was from a telemarketer. If it wasn't, usually the calling party will leave a message and nothing was lost by not answering.

Occasionally, we'll experience an especially determined telemarketer who continues to call back three or four times a day figuring that ultimately they will be connected to the target prospect. In such cases, what we do when we see the same calling number appear on the display is that we let the phone ring once or twice, then pick it up and hang up immediately without uttering a word into the phone. This is a very direct method of letting telemarketers know that theirs is an unwanted call and will not be answered no matter how many times they try.

Another option is to switch to an unlisted number, although some people must maintain a published number so that customers or clients can reach them. This is not recommended if you intend to operate your own business. If you do request to be unlisted, don't ask for a new phone number. You never know whose former phone number you're getting. Often, you're better off keeping your own.

It should be noted that what you've read in this chapter mostly applies to persons who maintain a landline phone. If you operate using only a mobile phone, it's unlikely that you'll experience the same problems with telemarketers.

You'll find more details about using a large display caller ID unit in Chapter 160.

134.

Veterans Benefits

If you have served in the military and are entitled to veterans status, you are entitled to many valuable benefits.

For those readers who aren't already familiar with this subject, take note that the Veterans Administration provides medical care, hospital care and prescription medications for all veterans who qualify. Depending on income, medical care is provided on a sliding scale down to practically zero for those veterans who are unemployed or without substantial assets.

If you are a veteran and not already in possession of a VA identification card, you should contact the nearest VA office or other VA facility and ask for the location nearest to you where you can apply for one.

A word of caution: Be prepared to wait when you go to apply. Many VA facilities are overburdened, so a wait of more than an hour is not unusual. Take a good book to read.

After your interview, the VA representative will be in a position to inform you of your medical care eligibility and possibly answer your questions about other veterans benefits. If not, you will be directed to the appropriate office.

In addition to medical care, the VA provides low-cost home mortgage loan guarantees and pays a substantial portion of college tuition, books, materials and one-on-one tutoring.

There are also additional benefits for students, and that means students of all ages. Best of all, your veterans benefits never expire.

When I was 36 years old, I returned to college to get a degree and continue on to an advanced degree. During that time, the VA paid for my tuition, textbooks and tutoring when required. It also paid for most of my child support.

If you aren't already fully informed, ask a friend or acquaintance who is making use of his/her veterans benefits and get an overview of all available benefits. In some instances, you might find that you are eligible to shop at a nearby post or base commissary, depending on your years and type of service.

You might be surprised what other benefits you might discover.

> **I have learned to seek my happiness by limiting my desires, rather than in attempting to satisfy them.**
>
> ***– John Stuart Mill***

135.

The Bank of George

Many owners of small-businesses share common problems — how to obtain a loan to expand their business or meet short-term cash needs.

Most banks aren't really interested in loaning money to fledgling new-business owners, especially home-based businesses.

As a result, many people in this predicament go from lender to lender, frustrated by waiting and red tape and, in the end, not getting their loan. They then do the worst thing possible — borrow cash on credit cards that carry interest rates of up to 21 percent. Do not do this. Period.

I solved this problem by becoming my own banker when "The Bank of George" was founded.

During one year, instead of buying a new car or going on a vacation, I lived austerely and saved every penny until I accumulated a nest egg of $5,000. In those days, $5,000 is what $10,000 to $20,000 is today.

I put every spare nickel into my business account with a red-lined "Hands Off!" That warning was for myself.

The "Bank of George" money I'd saved was used *only* for paying my creditors while awaiting payment from my customers which sometimes required from 30 to 45 days.

As soon as the customer paid me, the amount I'd "borrowed" went right back into this special account. It was *never* used for any other purpose, and it solved my monthly cash flow problem without ever needing to pay anyone a penny in interest.

In fact, the amount of interest I paid for business loans during the entire 18 years I produced newsletters? Zero.

The worry and frustration I experienced in connection with business loans? Zero.

A side benefit was that my vendors loved to do business with me because I always paid their bills the *same day* that I received them. Can you imagine anyone doing that today?

So, it came as no surprise that my vendors never hesitated for a moment when I asked for a special favor. And they always kept their prices low for me.

> **I think frugality drives innovation, just like other constraints do. One of the only ways to get out of a tight box is to invent your way out.**
>
> ***– Jeff Bezos***

136.

"Showrooming"

Wikipedia defines showrooming as the practice of examining merchandise in a traditional brick and mortar retail store without purchasing it, but then shopping online to find a lower price for the same item.

Showrooming has exacted a heavy toll on many big box discount stores. No longer do customers look for the product they are seeking and then buy. Instead, they pull out of their pocket their smartphones and begin to search the Internet for the lowest price on the item, whether it be a TV set, tablet or camera.

They might even ask a salesperson for a demonstration or ask questions about the product before heading out the door without making a purchase.

Once they're at home, they order the product online at the lowest cost available.

I'd like to say that I shed a tear for these big corporations whose existence is threatened by this trend. But, I remember that these are the same big box stores that are responsible for the closure of numerous family-owned camera and appliance stores.

There was a very fine such store in our city, one which welcomed returning customers and often let them know how much their business was appreciated, either in the form of extraordinary service or a discounted price.

But, since all of that falls into the category of history, let's move on and acknowledge that showrooming can save you money.

Occasionally, you'll find that the prices of some products or appliances are set by the manufacturer and it doesn't matter from which retailer you buy.

However, in most cases the prices of such products can often be found in a wide range.

You might land on the site of a retailer who has an overstock of the product you are seeking and wants to move it and offers a deep discount. Other times there might be a three-day sale on all merchandise that you order from a particular retailer.

If you opt to take that route, be sure you search and search until you come up with the best deal. That includes not only the price you are paying but also whether you can get free shipping and whether the product can be shipped to you by a retailer who is exempt from collecting sales tax, depending on where you live.

Remember, it's the entire deal that counts, not just the price of the item.

And a final tip — before completing the transaction online, go to Google and in the search box enter the name of the retail company or the product you are buying followed by the words "coupons" or "coupon codes."

If you are fortunate enough to locate a valid code, try entering it in the "Enter Coupon Code" or "Promo Code" box that appears when you check out at the site where you are buying your product. Often, you can get lucky and find a code for free shipping or a five or ten percent discount. That, too, should be considered as part of the total deal. More details on coupon codes and promo codes in Chapters 100 and 121.

137.

Save on Paper

My wife came upon this little strategy to save on paper costs. Add to that costly computer printer ink refills.

To save on paper, she recycles any sheet of 8½ x 11 computer printer paper that has been printed only on one side.

She simply turns it over to the unprinted side and stores these sheets in an office tray that is placed conveniently next to the printer.

When she prints copy that won't be leaving our home, she loads these recycled sheets into the printer tray and uses them exclusively for internal consumption.

We have need for a lot of this type of printing because like many others we don't like reading lengthy texts online and instead prefer to read it on hard copy (paper). We're referring to online texts that run a full page or more.

When both sides of the paper have been used, we toss them into our recycle bin which is picked up by city sanitation separate from trash and garbage. So, we're also doing our part for conservation.

An additional savings to this strategy is that on our inkjet printer, we switch the printer setting to "grayscale" whenever we want to print online pages. Grayscale is the most economical printer setting. It instructs the printer to print only in black ink and at the same time use the minimum amount.

By eliminating the various colors that might appear on the online page(s), you save even more as normally you wouldn't have a need for colored inks on pages that you have printed purely for your own informational purposes.

And if you are using a black-ink-only laser printer, you won't have that concern.

Remember that manufacturers of inkjet printers make little or no money on the sale of a new printer. They rely on your purchase of ink refills to bring in their profits.

> **Every time I am tempted to buy some dopey thing, I hear my late father's voice: 'Do you really need that?' He was big on saving money and buying as much security as possible. He also encouraged charitable giving. So, I am responsible with currency.**
>
> ***– Bill O'Reilly***

138.

Paper Towel Savings

While we're on the subject of paper, here's another great savings if you use paper towels in your kitchen, bathroom or garage workshop.

Bounty brand paper towels were the first to introduce Select-a-Size, and now it seems that all the other paper towel producers have climbed on board.

Select-a-Size towels are perforated for easy tearing every six inches instead of the customary twelve inches.

This enables consumers who don't require a large twelve-inch sheet to tear off a smaller six-inch sheet for their immediate need.

By doing this, you can be thrifty but still enjoy the convenience of using paper towels in your home.

My wife discovered these paper towels a few years ago and we've been using them ever since. I find that about nine out of ten times I'll tear off a six-inch sheet for my use and it will do the job with no problem. I don't need the twelve-inch sheet.

We eat at home mostly and so have a greater need for using paper towels than perhaps other households.

It's difficult to place a dollar figure on our annual paper towel savings, but I would estimate that our annual paper towel consumption has been cut in half.

A word of caution: Not all Bounty paper towels come in Select-a-Size format. The manufacturer continues to also offer standard-size formats and rolls. So be careful when you pick up a roll at the store. Make sure it's the size and style you want.

To get the very best deal, look for Bounty Select-a-Size in what its manufacturer designates the *Huge* size. To date, the only store where we have found Bounty Select-a-Size *Huge*-size rolls is at Target. If you sign up for a Target Red Card charge account, you'll save an additional five percent on almost anything you buy in the store, including the Select-a-Size paper towels.

Sometimes, just for fun, you might want to compute your percentage of savings when you compare the per square inch cost for what you are paying for paper towels with a competing quality towel that you would purchase at a major grocery chain in a standard-size roll without benefit of discount and a *Huge*-size roll at a discounted price.

Those who might scoff at these savings do not perhaps take into account that savings on this product occurs 24/7 and 365 days a year.

> **Debt is dumb. Cash is king.**
>
> ***– Dave Ramsey***

139.

Wear Out Your Clothes

I don't know exactly what the average individual spends on clothing, but I can assure you that I spend a lot less. The money I save is put to better use.

On this subject, it's important to emphasize that much like everything else we've been talking about, you must rid yourself of the belief that it's necessary or desirable to keep up with the Joneses. Instead, keep foremost in you thoughts the survival mindset of which we spoke earlier in this book. Your goal is to survive, and to do that you can't expect that you can live life and maintain the same lifestyle that you did when you were working at a steady job with a regular paycheck.

At the same time, there's no need to clothe yourself as if you are waiting in line outside a soup kitchen.

When I'm at home or just need to run out to the grocery store or bank, I wear what my wife refers to as my "uniform." It consists of a blue chambray work shirt and cotton khaki pants. These are both machine washable and can be worn more than once if necessary.

These are clothes that I normally wouldn't wear if I were going out to call on a customer or for any other business appointment. But, I wear these old clothes around the house until they are no longer wearable. At that point, they are discarded and used for cleaning rags.

When I go out on business, I wear more presentable-looking clothes appropriate for the occasion.

I buy most of my clothes and shoes online. I have no time to chase around to department stores and then not find what I'm seeking. Most of my clothing is purchased from L. L. Bean or

Land's End. Remember, your time is important, and much can be wasted making futile shopping trips to department stores.

As a general rule, I try to get full use out of everything I buy. I use it or wear it until it's no longer serviceable. That includes appliances, motor vehicles, etc. Learn to disregard any snide comments from your friends and acquaintances. They're not paying your bills. Perhaps, someday they'll come to you for advice when it's their turn to hit the unemployment line.

> **If you don't save the penny, you'll not have the dollar.**
>
> ***– Yiddish saying***

140.

Need a New Car? Really?

Once when I drove to the home of one of our renters who I'll call Brent — that wasn't his real name — I experienced one of the most satisfying moments I can recall.

Here's what happened: Brent and his family had moved into the three-bedroom, two-bath rental house only a few months prior, and I had spoken to Brent on the phone several times since then. We had some long conversations about economic survival in the tough economy. It was obvious to me that Brent was a kindred spirit when it came to "dollars and sense."

Brent was in his thirties, energetic, hard-working and was employed in a mid-level job at a large corporation.

In his spare time, he and a friend had invested in a fixer-upper house and flipped it at the right moment. Of course, that was before the sub-prime mortgage debacle and subsequent stock market crash.

He chose to rent instead of buying his own house so that he could have more available cash to put into his own growing real estate investments.

On the day that I drove to his house, it was for the purpose of inspecting a worn kitchen appliance that needed replacement. I was also eager to talk with him as a result of our previous phone conversations as I believed we'd have a lot in common.

I parked on the street in front of the house and as he came out to greet me I noticed he had a huge smile on his face. He quickly escorted me into the house where his wife was waiting in the doorway.

At that moment, he let out a guffaw, slapped his knee, and still smiling with glee pointed his finger back toward my car, then at his wife and proudly bellowed "I told you so!"

It took me only a moment to figure out that he had earlier predicted that I would not be driving a late model luxury car, and he had been proven right.

In fact I was driving a 30-year-old economy car that my mother had bought five years before she passed away in 1987.

Well, I'm still driving that same car today and it runs well.

When we plan a car trip, we rent a new car, of course at discount rates. What we've saved on new car payments, interest, insurance costs, higher license plate fees — my fee is only $21.00 a year — gas, etc., I can use toward the purchase of income property.

Not long ago, I came across data showing that if you buy a new car every ten years, instead of every three years, you'll save $250,000 to $300,000 in your lifetime. And if you're a young person reading this, the figure might reach $500,000.

My friends often ask me when I'll be buying a new car and my answer remains the same: "When the old one gives up the ghost."

One of those friends owns a Mercedes, and a simple lube and oil change costs him around $300.00. Mine costs $19.00.

> **Frugality is founded on the principal that all riches have limits.**
>
> **– Edmund Burke**

141.

Haircuts

Haircuts can cost you anywhere from eight or nine dollars for a cheapie up to the sky's-the-limit if you go to a top-flight stylist.

If you have a relative or friend who can cut hair, you can save significantly.

For many years when things were financially tight, my wife cut my hair. We figured that saved close to $150 a year and no one could tell the difference.

Unfortunately, I didn't have the necessary skills to cut her hair.

This is simply another example how you and your family can save money when you are trying to get by on a drastically-reduced income.

You won't need to do this for the rest of your life. Once your business is established and you have a comfortable income stream, you can relax some of the austerity measures and allow yourself to indulge a bit.

> **Most of America's millionaires buy used cars.**
>
> ***– The Millionaire Next Door***

142.

Dry Cleaning

Having your everyday clothes dry cleaned is a lot more expensive than dropping them into your clothes washer at home or at a Laundromat.

For that reason, I try to buy washable clothes for almost every need and season.

Of course, there are some events where washable clothes just aren't appropriate, and in those instances I do wear clothing made of fabrics that require dry cleaning.

I would estimate that I make perhaps one or two trips a year to the dry cleaners and the total cost never exceeds twenty dollars.

Remember, it all adds up.

> **There's no such thing as a free lunch.**
>
> ***– Milton Friedman***

143.

Rx Medicines for Your Pets

If your pet or pets require ongoing medication for a chronic problem or disorder, listen up.

No. I'm not going to point you to those TV commercials advertising low-cost pet medications via mail. Being a pet owner, I have checked these out and too often found that the prices offered by online sites are not much different than those charged by veterinarians if you have your pet's prescription filled in the vet's office. I once ordered from one of these companies and found that the difference in price was minuscule.

But, here's the good news. There are at least two sources — and perhaps more — where you can purchase prescription medicines for your pets at substantial savings.

It's not made easy, however.

First, no supplier can provide you with any meds unless you already have a prescription from a veterinarian. And sometimes getting one can be difficult.

Here's why: In many instances, to operate a veterinary office or clinic as a successful business, your vet needs to make a profit from a combination of fees including office visits, examinations, treatments, filling medication prescriptions and selling prescription pet foods.

Often the percentage of markup on prescription medications is quite high. Sometimes it can be four or five times the price you would be charged at a discount pharmacy, at the same time keeping in mind that the discount provider is still making a profit, though admittedly a modest one.

A friend who recently learned of these alternative sources asked his vet for a written prescription. The vet responded by asking my friend why he wanted a written prescriptions since the medications were available in his clinic.

My friend answered honestly that he wanted to buy the prescribed medications from a source which offered lower prices.

The vet appeared displeased, but couldn't refuse the request because to do so would place him in violation of various state laws and regulations. He ended up handing my friend the requested written prescriptions which my friend later filled at one of the discount sources.

How a request of this type is handled can be a touchy issue and holds the potential to create a strained relationship between you and your vet.

If your pet comes down with an acute condition which requires perhaps only one-time treatment, then, of course, it doesn't make sense to push for a written prescription and fill it elsewhere. You could burn your bridges with your vet by doing so.

But, if your pet needs a prescription filled ongoing, perhaps year after year, and the cost is high, then it makes sense to shop for alternative sources.

One way is to try to get a cooperative vet to write you a prescription either for a year's supply of the medication or what is known as a PRN, which stands for *pro re nata* and means that it can be refilled as needed, often up to one year. This way you can order a year's supply and often beyond and save on shipping costs.

One pet owner with whom I'm acquainted found a vet who makes house calls and does not have his own medication dispensary. He had no reluctance to write prescriptions, knowing that doing so would not diminish his income.

All of this will undoubtedly require laying out a strategy on your part. Once you have your ducks in order, the two sources that I've had experience with are Costco and Lambert Vet Supply. The former needs no introduction. Lambert is located in Kansas and

Nebraska and owns and operates its own pharmacy in addition to selling non-prescription vet supplies at its two locations.

Costco recently began providing pet medicines, but from my own experience they don't always have every medication available.

Lambert, which has an online presence, stocks almost every medication.

Again, to access these sources of pet meds requires careful planning and a good amount of diplomacy. Remember, your objective is to save money, not to alienate your pet's vet.

> **A bargain ain't a bargain unless it's something you need.**
>
> ***– Sidney Carroll***

144.

Regifting

These items were formerly referred to as "floating gifts," but now the more modern terminology is "regifting." Doing regifting can save you money, but be careful.

I mentioned in an earlier chapter that you can save money by making your own gifts. However, you might also choose to make use of gifts you've received that you don't want by regifting them to another person and save money in the process.

From what I've been told by those who do this regularly is that the key to success as well as avoiding embarrassment is tagging every unwanted gift that comes into your home. Then storing these floating gifts in a central location outside the view of any visitors who might come into your home.

Failure to do this can result in serious consequences and possibly the loss of a friend or acquaintance.

When a gift comes in that you don't want or can't use, write out a tag showing the name of the giver and the date. Then place it in an out-of-the way location together with all other collected floating gifts.

Then when an occasion arises where you believe it is appropriate to bring a small gift, look among your collected floating gifts to see if you have something that will fit the occasion.

Once you've landed upon the right item, make sure that (1) you're not giving it back to the person who gave it to you, or (2) that you're not giving it to someone who is acquainted with the original giver.

Often it's safer to send the item to someone distant and for whom it would be impossible to be connected with the giver since that person lives in another city and would not know the giver, assuming that such is the case.

It's only my opinion, but I believe regifting is appropriate when a small gift is called for, but not for a major event such as a wedding, anniversary, etc.

Again, if you do this, you must exercise caution.

> **No man is rich enough to waste his money in putting on style.**
>
> ***– Gustavits F. Swift***

145.

Do You Really Need Two Cars?

For many of us, we've grown accustomed to every member of the household having his/her own car.

In a robust economy, that's been an affordable option and we haven't questioned it.

But, if your job has disappeared or your income has been reduced, then these aren't normal times. When you suddenly find yourself in stressed economic circumstances, the smart thing to do is look around and see where you can cut expenses.

And to borrow a familiar quote from national leaders past and present, "All options are on the table."

This means, you need to do this, too. Nothing can remain sacrosanct.

Obviously, if you are a two-vehicle couple and both of you have full-time jobs located miles away in diametrically opposite directions, then perhaps you have no other alternative but to continue operating both vehicles.

However, if you can figure out logistically how you can get by with one vehicle, you can save thousands of dollars a year.

You'll need to do some smart planning, because this is yet another challenge that will test your ability to surmount obstacles which appear in your path.

What you will save on monthly payments, gasoline, insurance, license plate fees, etc., will provide you with additional cash as well as peace of mind and a lessening of worries about "How am I going to pay those bills?"

You'll sleep better, too.

146.

Smartphones vs. Smart Consumers

While many of my friends can't wait to get their hands on the latest electronic gadgets, such as Smartphones, etc., I can't wait to get on with my work and leave the gadgets and games to those who seem to have more leisure time and extra money to spend on amusements.

Included among these gadgets are the various generations of the so-called Smartphones.

Do they perform as their promotions claim? In most cases, absolutely.

Do I need the latest version of a Smartphone with all the bells and whistles? Answer: No.

Certainly there are instances where a Smartphone or tablet is essential to someone's work or daily responsibilities. In such cases, these devices can prove a blessing, saving both time and money.

But, if you don't have a specific need for them, why lay out a hundred dollars a month — or more — for service plus the initial cost of several hundred dollars for the phone itself?

My money-saving approach is to use a cheap cellphone — purchase price under fifty dollars — and load it with prepaid minutes which I buy from the provider offering the lowest cost.

Such a cellphone meets my needs just fine, that being to make and receive calls when I'm away from my home landline.

Recently, my cellphone provider increased its rates substantially for prepaid minutes, perhaps a way of saying that the company didn't see much profit in selling prepaid minutes.

I decided to cancel and move on.

As my luck would have it, I walked into a Target store on a quiet weekday afternoon.

Once inside the store's electronics section, I was approached by a friendly young man who was both bright and well informed about the various low-cost cellphone plans available.

Within moments he grasped what I was looking for and began showing me an assortment of low-cost cellphones and accompanying prepaid minutes packages.

Although it might seem hard to believe, when I walked out of the store with a new cellphone in my hand, I was afraid that the police might suddenly tap me on the shoulder because the price was *so low.*

Backing up in my story, after a length of time, the young salesman took me to a TracFone instrument. The price? Only $4.99. It was a basic simple model that allowed me to make and receive calls (no Smartphone capabilities).

I also bought 60 prepaid minutes which would have expired in a few months, either 60 or 90 days, I can't remember exactly.

When it came time for the salesman to process my order, he advised me that there was a storewide sale in progress that reduced the cost of my entire purchase by 10 percent.

Next, he pulled out his own Smartphone and brought up the TracFone website where he was able to access yet an additional promotional savings.

At checkout, I paid for my purchase using a Target Red Card (Target's own credit card) and walked out the door with my new phone and 60 prepaid minutes for a total purchase price that was just under $25.00.

And there were more savings. I learned that when activating my new phone, the salesman had taken advantage of a special promotion that extended the expiration date of my minutes from 60 days to a full six months.

In my hand I had a new cellphone with six months to use up 60 prepaid minutes. No monthly charges and no long list of added surtaxes and services charges.

Oh, and there is no monthly bill either. You are just charged for the prepaid minutes. That's all.

For someone like me, who doesn't text and doesn't live on his cellphone, my monthly cost for cellphone service is now about $4.00 a month. What are you paying for your service?

Further, I would swear on a stack of bibles that I can't recall a single instance in the last ten years when I felt that I needed a Smartphone and wished that I had one.

I admit that I'm not the average guy when it comes to cellphone needs.

Frankly, I don't have time to spend entertaining myself on a Smartphone or texting my friends. I have a small business to run and there exists a need to eat, sleep, work and survive.

If you are committed to cutting all but essential expenses to the bone, this is a good place to start.

> **Industry is fortune's right hand,**
> **and frugality its left.**
>
> ***– John Ray***

147.

Does Anyone Save Anymore?

Americans today are among the worst savers in the world. One study shows that our average savings rate is on the negative side of the chart. In other words, as a nation, we spend more than we earn.

I can't remember what motivated me, but as a young man, I decided that it was better to live below my means. The motivation might have stemmed from an experience I had while working as a temporary employee on a county government survey crew.

One day at lunch, I heard an older man, who was part of our team, tell an acquaintance why he was working at such a menial job. He explained that two years earlier, working as a real estate agent, he'd earned $60,000 and began to live like someone making $60,000. Adjusted for inflation, that would amount to at least $180,000 in today's economy.

The next year, he said, due to a downturn in the real estate market, he earned only $6,000 and lost everything — his house, vacation condo and the new Mercedes.

A change in fortune like this can happen to anyone, especially in an unstable economy, as some of us well know.

Another time, I worked with a man who seemed untroubled about having bills far in excess of his ability to pay. I once asked him whether being in debt didn't worry him.

He laughed and shook his head. "I don't worry, he said. "I let my creditors worry."

The reverse side of this coin — having savings in reserve for a rainy day — enables you to say "no" to a boss or "no" to a customer.

This is when the request is unacceptable or the job is not one you think it wise to take, you won't suffer because of the lack of income since your rainy day savings will see you through.

Needless to say, most of us won't have those resources available if we, at the same time, try to maintain a lifestyle affordable to only the rich and famous.

Admittedly, this calls for an amount of self-discipline as do many of the other recommendations found in this book.

And in order to save money for emergencies and for the future, you'll need to also master some life changes such as time management, living within or below your means, frugality and freedom from indebtedness, to name a few.

However, you know and I know that thousands before us have gladly traded the chains of their former lifestyles for the freedom which self-employment offers despite the hard work, long hours and sacrifice.

> **There is no dignity quite so impressive,**
> **and no independence quite so important,**
> **as living within your means.**
>
> ***– Calvin Coolidge***

148.

Manager's Special

The next time you're grocery shopping, check out the meat and seafood section for anything tagged "Manager's Special."

Usually, these items are not advertised specials or club specials but perishables approaching their "sell by" or "use by" date and must be sharply discounted to assure immediate sale.

Before buying one of these "manager's specials," I follow these two rules: (1) I make contact and get on a friendly basis with one of the employees in the meat department and won't consider making a purchase until I've spoken with that person and asked why it's discounted; (2) I will only consider buying the item if I can use it that same day. I'm not interested in freezing meat or fish nearing its pull date. I want a bargain, not a trip to urgent care.

Although there are always exceptions, usually you'll find that a reputable grocery chain won't risk selling an over-the-hill item as a manager's special

A friend, who fancies steaks, often buys them for half-price when they are on a manager's special. He shops on the way home from the gym and then broils the steak for dinner that same night. His savings on the entrée allows him to enjoy a half bottle of cabernet along with his steak.

149.

Biggest Entertainment Bargain

The biggest entertainment bargain in America, hands down, is Netflix.

For about $10.00 a month (subject to price change) you can subscribe your family to Netflix streaming. This service is available if you are connected to the Internet and have a player to project the movies onto your TV.

For about the same price you can subscribe to Netflix's disc service. The only disadvantage is that the service isn't instant as it is on streaming. You must wait for the day's mail to arrive. The advantages are that the film selection is much wider and includes recent releases and Oscar winners. Also, there won't be instances of either Internet slowdowns or buffering.

Having tried both, we prefer Netflix movies to be mailed to us, mainly because of a wider selection of available films and never having our viewing interrupted by technical problems, such as buffering or other Internet slowdowns.

If you are into saving money, getting quality entertainment and watching your choice of movies sans commercials, and all that without having to leave your house — this is it. And if you are, for example, a family of four, imagine viewing a first-run movie in your home at a cost of only about 50 cents per person.

Make your own popcorn from scratch and save an additional ten dollars or more.

You can't beat Netflix.

150.

Free Computer Access

If times are really tough and there's no money available for a computer or a connection to the Internet, consider this option.

Go to your neighborhood's public library and use the computers there. It's free.

Most public libraries will allow you up to one hour of online computer use. You must usually sign in and sometimes wait if a computer isn't immediately available. Some libraries allow you to reserve a computer at a certain hour so you can count on one being available at a time convenient for you.

Many libraries offer the opportunity to print pages that you select at a cost of about 10 cents a copy. To save money, come equipped with a pen and note pad and jot down pertinent information that you need to take home with you and avoid the printing cost.

You can both send and receive email from most library computers.

Try to remain businesslike and establish a good reputation with the librarians responsible for assigning computers to library patrons. It will help you to more readily secure computer use in the future.

And here's a tip: Don't plan your visit to the library right after school lets out. Once the kids get out of class and descend on the library, it's often a case of pandemonium. You don't need that.

If you're going in summer when the kids are out of school, make plans to go when the library first opens in the morning. Kids don't like to get up early if they don't have to, and early will be your opportunity. You're more likely to have a quiet experience if you do that.

151.

Buy "In Season"

Perhaps, in the past, you didn't pay much attention to which foods were in season. If you wanted to prepare asparagus for dinner, it didn't matter whether the price was $1.29 a pound or $4.89 a pound. You had the income and you bought what you had a yen for eating.

Today, with the realities of "the new normal" staring you in the face, things may be quite different.

But, take heart. You can still enjoy the bounty of fresh food. You'll just need to synchronize your tastes with your pocketbook.

For example, throughout the summer our nearby supermarket usually features fresh peaches and nectarines at the special price of 99 cents a pound.

Not only can you enjoy eating fresh fruit throughout the summer months, but at these prices it pays to either freeze or can some of these fruits.

In October, you'll find the lowest prices for apples which are in season at that time of year or citrus which comes in season in winter.

"In season" also applies to fresh vegetables and fish, particularly salmon.

Once you become familiar with the different "in season" cycles, you can plan ahead for your meals and, of course, save money in doing so.

What's more, eating fresh food in season is much tastier than canned or frozen and according to experts it's better for your health.

152.

When Money is Really Tight

During one of the worst periods of the Great Recession, I recall watching a newscast in which a middle-aged woman was shown walking out of her local food bank with a large bag of groceries.

She told a TV news reporter on the street that only a year earlier she was a volunteer working on the *other side* of the counter handing out canned goods to those in need.

However, in the last year both she and her husband had lost good-paying jobs and were facing foreclosure on their house.

How quickly things can change, she noted sadly.

If you currently find yourself at such a point, and things have hit bottom for you and your family, you shouldn't hesitate to avail yourself of the resources of this safety net.

A major plank in the survival mindset to which I frequently refer in this book is that you can't allow pride to get in the way of your financial recovery. If ownership of a successful sewer and drain cleaning service is the key to your economic independence, for example, you need to be able to hold your head high when you're among your friends, regardless of the fact that they may still be clinging to their six-figure positions.

If they're really your friends, they will understand, if for no other reason than next month it could be them.

So, accept groceries from the food bank as long as you need them. And once you've recovered financially you can be either a volunteer or a donor to that same food bank. What's that old saying? *What goes around comes around.*

Take when help is offered and give back when you're able.

153.

Bigger Isn't Always Better

I learned when I was a youngster that bigger isn't always better. During summers, I bought peaches, plums, grapes and cherries when I wanted something sweet (I didn't like candy). I quickly discovered that the higher-priced, larger pieces of fruit didn't taste any better than the smaller pieces. In fact, they were often not as sweet or juicy.

I've seen grocery stores sell large grapefruit for $1.29 per pound and slightly smaller ones for 39 cents a pound. This tells me that buyers want big pieces of fruit, so stores must increase the price on the larger pieces and cut the price on the smaller ones to balance supply and demand.

Often the best buy on apples or oranges are those that come in a plastic bag weighing three pounds. The price per pound for these is substantially less than that charged for the larger pieces which you select individually. The same rule applies to many other foods and products.

Because I enjoy fruit that's sweet and has character, I always search the produce bins for all the ripe fruit that I can find. Frequently, that applies to smaller-size fruits.

If saving money is wrong,
I don't want to be right!

– William Shatner

154.

The High Cost of Smoking

Are you a smoker?

I'll spare you the lecture on how it affects your health because you've already heard it a thousand times.

But, what about the financial cost? Nowadays a carton of cigarettes can cost as much as $87.50. That will buy a lot of groceries or fill your car's gas tank two or three times.

Beyond that, if you expect to be a success in business — unless you intend to confine your business to exclusively mail order — your customers, unless they are smokers themselves, won't be comfortable doing face-to-face business with you. They might not say anything about it to you, but if you don't hear from them again, smoking could be the reason.

Even if you don't smoke in their presence, they can smell the smoke on your clothes, your hair or on your breath.

Trust me on this. I've had it told to me about others (in confidence) several times. And I'm not a smoker.

> **The wisdom of life consists in the elimination of nonessentials.**
>
> ***– Lin Yutang***

155.

Airline Tickets

If you fly often, you know that there are always several prices for the same seat or destination. The trick is to catch the best price, and that's not easy.

According to published research, the best time to buy a ticket is 54 days prior to your departure date. Tickets are typically at the lowest price then.

But, to be sure you're getting the lowest price before you click on "buy," you'll need to do some further investigation. This requires an online search of several travel websites including that of the airline. Then, phoning the airline's central reservations 800 number and getting a quote. Then going back and checking a few more websites, and finally calling the airline's central reservations number and restating your request. You will undoubtedly be talking to different reservations agents who might come up with yet another quote which is different from ones you've previously been quoted.

You won't know for sure if you're getting the lowest price until you've done all the above. Yes, it's a bit time consuming and often frustrating, but why pay more if you can get a cheaper fare?

Another tip: If your area is served by Southwest Airlines, be sure to check their prices. A little-known fact is that many of the travel websites don't include Southwest in their computer searches, so you'll need to contact them or go to their website.

Finally, once you have what appears to be the lowest price, phone the airline's central reservations again and ask if you would be charged an extra fee for making your reservation and buying your ticket via telephone. If so, buy your ticket online.

Sometimes, when making a complicated reservation, it's not possible to purchase your ticket online. In that case, phone and ask the reservations agent if an exception can be made to imposing an added fee since it's impossible to buy the ticket you want online.

Also be sure to find out the airline's fees for checked baggage and carry-ons. Better to know in advance than be surprised at the check-in counter and be told your flight's going to cost you another $50.00 each way.

Wealth can only be accumulated by the earnings of industry and the savings of frugality.

– John Tyler

156.

Online Promo Codes

If you are like me and make most of your purchases on the Internet to save time, money and avoid sales tax, don't overlook one more important money saver that is often missed. That's a special promotion code that entitles you to a discount.

When I make an online purchase, this is how I proceed: First, I enter the name of the product along with a model number if needed. Then, I add these words in the Google search box: "lowest price."

Usually, Google will bring up quite a number of links to the exact item you are seeking. You then need to ferret out the seller that is offering the best deal. You'll also need to check the seller's track record for reliability. Yelp.com can often help with that. Also, you can look up the seller's rating on the Better Business Bureau's website.

Once you've decided from which company you're going to buy the product, you'll need to see if you can find a discount promo code for that company.

You do that by going to either one of these two websites which have been previously mentioned in this book:

www.retailmenot.com

www.couponcabin.com

Then enter the name of the company under consideration in the website's search box.

Most often, these websites will have a listing for the company you're searching and will offer several promo codes. You might find one that offers free shipping while another will give you a five percent discount on all purchases. Others will offer a discount only on certain sale items. Sometimes, a promo code has expired.

But, it costs nothing to try.

Another approach is to go back to Google and enter, for example, XYZ Company and the words "promo code."

When you do that, you never know what you're going to find. Lots of websites will pop up and many, you'll find, simply don't deliver what they promise. They'll make you jump through numerous hoops, sign up for their service or promotions and leave you still waiting for the coupon or promo code that you thought you were going to get.

All that said, I would estimate that I find a usable promo code for almost half of my online purchases. And that's not hay. It's real money saved.

Another strategy is to buy in quantity. Sometimes you will receive additional discounts if you're buying a product, such as a vitamin or a supplement that you consume regularly, so long as there's no concern of spoilage, etc.

If you're making a purchase from Amazon, don't expect to find a promo code. I cannot recall ever having seen one. However, Amazon often offers free shipping on purchases of $35.00 or more, which sometimes makes it a better deal than the other guy's.

157.

The Art of Bargaining

There's a time and a place to haggle over price, and I learned about it reading my *Consumer Reports.*

According to the publication, consumers can be very effective in reducing prices on major purchases, such as appliances, if they engage in bargaining.

However, don't expect success if you attempt to bargain at a chain-owned business, particularly a national chain such as Sears, Best Buy, Walmart or Costco. Sales staffs at these chains and others rarely have authority to make deals.

But, at an independently-owned business, especially if you are speaking directly with the owner, you can usually benefit from bargaining.

The results of the *Consumer Reports* study suggest that you try bargaining if you are prepared to buy more than one big ticket item.

For instance, let's say that you have recently moved, have no furniture or appliances and you are inside an independently-owned store that specializes in new or used furniture and appliances.

If you pick out several pieces, including, let's say, a refrigerator, microwave, TV and a bed and you ask if you can get a break if you buy all those pieces, you are a good candidate to receive a significant discount.

Should the salesperson fail to accommodate your request, ask immediately to speak with either the owner or the manager.

Sometimes a salesperson might not care if you buy or not, but you can be sure that an owner or manager won't want to see you walk out the door without making a purchase.

If you choose the right store and the right conditions, bargaining can result in substantial savings for you.

158.

There's No Tax on Saving Money

To my knowledge, there is no tax on the money you've saved by not spending it.

If you save $100 at the supermarket this month by buying specials, that's $100 in your pocket to spend for something else or to simply save.

Consider this: If you wanted to put $100 into your savings account at the bank and you had to first earn the money, you might need to earn $125 or $135 and pay the various income taxes before you had $100 that you could then put into your savings account.

This might seem pretty basic to some, but it's an economic reality that many of us sometimes overlook.

Meanwhile, some states require their residents to pay a use tax on any item purchased outside the state in which they reside and on which they haven't already paid a state sales tax.

With more types of income being taxed, such as when you sell a used item on eBay or at a garage sale, it's indeed comforting to know that you don't need to pay tax on the money you've saved.

> **Never spend your money before you have earned it.**
>
> ***– Thomas Jefferson***

159.

Reduce Property Taxes

You should look into what your neighbors are paying in property taxes to determine if you are being assessed fairly, even if you don't suspect that yours are too high.

Property tax data is available online in almost every county, and it's a snap to log on and see the assessed values of houses in your immediate neighborhood.

This is even made easier if you live in a tract or subdivision where there are only a few different models. That allows you to compare apples to apples.

Suppose you live in a Model D unit and there are two neighbors on your block who also own Model D homes. Check their assessed valuations. They should be identical or very close to your own. That is unless they have a swimming pool or have added rooms to their property.

If your assessed valuation is higher than theirs, it's time to take action.

If after checking you believe that you have been over-assessed, you have a once-a-year opportunity to file an appeal with the county assessor. If that effort fails, you can usually request that your case be heard by an appeals board. Some states provide a further third level for appeal, often in court.

When you are writing your appeal, be sure to stick to facts. Use words such as "in fairness" or "equitability." Avoid emotional words or those that imply unfairness or favoritism. Also, talk to friends who have filed successful appeals.

A few minutes comparing your property taxes to those of your neighbors could save you hundreds of dollars every year.

160.

Caller ID — A Must

Caller Identification saves you time. That means it also saves you money.

Despite Congress' passage of the Do Not Call law, telemarketers have found that they can disregard the law and in recent years have ramped up with impunity. There are more telemarketer live and robot calls coming into our household today than ever before.

And every single one will steal your time away if you answer the call.

Since there's apparently little or no significant enforcement of the Do Not Call law, we've installed caller ID display units at each phone in the house, that is if the particular instrument isn't already equipped with one.

We pick up only calls from those telephone numbers or caller's names that we recognize and let our voicemail take the others.

In the kitchen/family room area, where we spend the greatest portion of our time, we've installed an oversize caller ID display device which we can easily read from anywhere in the room. It saves us from having to get up and go to the phone where there is a tiny caller ID device which sometimes requires eyeglasses to read. If you haven't discovered this technique already, you'll find that telemarketers won't waste *their* time leaving a message. So, there's nothing to play back, and that too is a time saver.

If we're knee deep in a project or working against a deadline, we'll wait to return legitimate calls after our work is finished, even if it's from a friend or relative.

Remember, your Prime Time is the time of the day when you need to address yourself to earning money and to nothing else. Allow no distractions!

161.

Are You Getting "Value"?

Whether you are making decisions in the role of a consumer or a business person, it's critical that you receive "value" for the expenditure of both your time and your money.

"Sure," you say. "Any fool knows that." But, maybe not. I know individuals who think nothing of driving 20 miles across town to take advantage of an advertised bargain on one or two relatively inexpensive items.

They will buy one item at a cost of $8.95, saving perhaps a couple dollars. They will not consider the fact that they've used a couple hours of their time and at least a gallon or two of gasoline. Perhaps, if they had stocked up and bought a dozen of the sale items, it might have made sense.

A service tech I know agreed to drive 30 miles to the next town to provide assistance to a customer whose computer had broken down. He didn't quote the customer either a fuel surcharge or trip charge and had obliged the customer by agreeing to a discounted price he requested. At day's end, he had invested approximately four hours of his time, burned several gallons of gasoline and returned home with a check in his pocket for $45.00. No value for his time spent or services rendered.

Whether it's a low price on an item you're buying or whether you are agreeing to perform a service or sell a product, before you make a decision you must calculate whether there is "value" in it for you.

And keep in mind, "value" doesn't always translate into money. You might be building goodwill with a customer and therefore willing to forfeit an immediate payoff, knowing that will come later. Your experience tells you that it's both wise and prudent to allow this particular customer a special discount or a free service... because, because, because. And in time this gesture will result in increased business or referral to a new customer. Your decision in this case is actually an investment in a likely "value" in the future.

Act like a startup. Forget about fancy offices, fast cars and fat expense accounts. Your wallet is your company's life-blood. Practice and perfect the art of being frugal. Watch every dollar and triple-check every expense. Maintain a low overhead and manage your cash flow effectively

– Scott D. Gerber

162.

Senior Discounts at Age 50?

Recently, a friend emailed me one of those lists that go around on the Internet containing the names of dozens of national chains which offer senior discounts. I'm not including the list in this book because as one knows, lists of this type are obsolete the day after they're issued.

Better that you go to Google and enter the words "senior discounts." There you will find numerous sites offering such lists in various forms and categories. These include discounts for restaurants, retail merchandise, travel, car rental, entertainment and more.

But, getting back to the key issue, that being the age at which senior discounts are offered by the different chains, I made some fascinating discoveries. Not all senior discounts require a minimum age of 65. Some start at age 50, others at 55 and some at 62.

Because it's expected that a large percentage of readers of this book will be middle age or older, this is yet another avenue for reducing expenses and yet not suffering the loss of certain previously-enjoyed extras.

As I eyeballed the extensive list of chains offering senior discounts, I noticed that many chains simply accept an AARP membership card to qualify for the discount.

When I checked in late December, 2015, I found that AARP membership cost $16.00 for one year and $63.00 for a five-year membership. That comes out to only $12.60 a year. Minimum age to join is 50.

So, if you're 50 or older you can join and get a membership card. Wherever you go or shop and they offer a senior discount, you can ask first if they accept AARP membership for senior discount. If the answer is yes, try showing the card and ask for the senior discount. In many cases, that may be all that's necessary. If you are asked to show proof of your age and you don't meet their specific age requirements, well, at least you've tried.

Some of the senior discounts offered might be only 10 percent. But some are substantial and are offered only on certain days of the week.

But, now here's the secret: Often you must *ask* for the senior discount. It won't be offered unless you *ask*. So speak up and save!

> **If you can, you will quickly find that the greatest rate of return you will earn is on your own personal spending. Being a smart shopper is the first step to getting rich.**
>
> ***– Mark Cuban***

163.

The Best Question

If you are vetting a project or are on any sort of fact-finding mission and in contact with a key person who holds the information you're seeking and you want to be sure that there isn't anything that you might have bypassed or overlooked, consider posing this question.

Before departing or concluding your phone conversation, pause for a moment, thank the person for their help, and then ask: "By the way, are there any questions that I *should* have asked you that I didn't ask?"

Asking this question when making a purchase, a reservation, an inquiry or facing a bureaucrat has saved me from making many mistakes because of incomplete information.

Try it. You, too, might be surprised at some of the responses.

Thrift is not an affair of the pocket,
but an affair of character.

– S.W. Straus

Extra Bonus

Although many folks I know don't place a high value on searching for just the right words in an awkward situation, I personally have found the careful use of language to be extremely helpful.

One powerful word that I have added to my vocabulary over the years, is the word "appropriate."

For example, you might be asked why you chose to buy a certain item or why you decided to select a certain person and you either can't immediately come up with an answer that will satisfy the questioner or you don't wish to be so candid, you simply reply, "I chose him because I felt he would be the appropriate person for the job."

Or "I selected this gift because I think it would be appropriate for Mark and Debbie."

From my experience, you can't go wrong when you use this word.

Another useful response to use when you wish to avoid controversy is, "What would you suggest?" I use this response when I encounter a very critical individual whom nothing seems to suit and it places the ball squarely in the other person's court. Then, I remain silent until he or she answers.

When you are in a situation where you are uncertain as to what exactly is on the mind of another person who is either a leader or seems to be in control and you don't want to misstep by taking the lead yourself or saying or asking something that might cause you to appear naïve or unsophisticated, you respond with these words, "How should we proceed?"

Finally, here's a response drawn from personal experience that I find myself using almost daily.

Because you can count on people reacting negatively when you say "no" to their requests, I try to never use it as a one-word answer.

Instead, if I find I can't accommodate an individual's request, I use a different response. I tell the person that I'd like to be able to say "yes" and I then provide an explanation as to why I can't do whatever was requested of me.

I picked this up from one of the more memorable characters I've known. He was the top official of a national organization whom I often had to contact in my work.

Before contacting him for the first time, I had heard through the grapevine that this man had a reputation for never saying "no." Sure enough, the first time I phoned him, and after hearing my request, he replied, "George, I'd like to be able to say 'yes,' but..." and then went on to tell me why he couldn't grant my request. For years, my office co-workers and I joked about this official's habit of never saying "no." But, it left an impression on all of us.

> **If you realize that you have enough,**
> **you are truly rich.**
>
> ***– Lao Tzu***

An Afterword

For those who have read through the book to this point, I hope that you are inspired and heartened by the knowledge that you *do* have a future ahead of you.

If you can cast aside the unhelpful desire to keep up with the Joneses; if you are a self-starter; then your chances of succeeding are well above average.

Reaching your goal of financial independence — regardless of the economic climate — depends largely on your ability to stay focused.

In simple terms, maintaining and developing your business comes first. Expect to put in 12-hour days or longer at the start. Whatever it takes.

When you're not stoking the fires of your business, you can devote time to figuring how you can save money and cut expenses. I've given you lots of ideas and when you visit some of the recommended websites you'll find more ideas. But, remember: Business first!

It all comes down to how you manage your time. If you manage it efficiently, you'll succeed. If you slack off and do what millions do — spend hours playing electronic games, watching mindless "entertainment" shows on TV or surfing the Internet — you'll be squandering not just valuable time, but your life. It's that survival mindset that gives you the edge over those who are not as focused or disciplined as you are.

Finally, it's important to have an idea of what you can expect of the economy in the next decade or beyond. When I chose the title for this book, I invoked the term *Upside Down Economy.* I did so because this is a term that all of us can easily understand.

What I really wanted to emphasize is that we live in what I see as a dysfunctional society. One without the economic base that is necessary for humans to be able to count on the basics for their everyday lives. And along with it comes the disappearance of the middle class.

The dysfunctionality begins in the home where a huge percentage of Americans find themselves in debt and it ends with their government invoking debt as a solution to budget shortages.

Add to the dysfunctionality in government and politics our government being unable to consider major issues facing us and elected officials so concerned with denigrating their opponents that they can hardly agree on any legislative actions short of those few that are critical to staving off major crises.

In my opinion, it will require key structural changes by which we manage our economy to reverse the current decline in our standard of living. To detail these changes and what brought us to this point would require a separate book.

So, I'll condense this to a sentence by predicting that the issue that will ultimately emerge will be that of *dysfunctionality vs. sustainability.*

You don't hear the word *sustainability* used often nowadays, with the exception perhaps of environmentalists or your kids or grandkids learning it in school. But, stay tuned. There are an increasing number of voices who are passionate advocates of sustainability and they will soon be bringing it to your door. Those in the vanguard are mostly young, bright and inspired.

And while I see sustainability as the ultimate solution, I don't see it being adopted as a long-term goal anytime soon.

So, if you want to succeed, you'll need to do it independently and by doing so bring about your own sustainability.

Trust me. It's possible. I've done it. And I've reached that age in life where I would like to pass on what I've learned to those who can benefit.

Good luck!

About the Author

George Newman was born in Vienna, Austria on August 26, 1936. Two years later, his family fled the Nazi annexation and came to the United States. He grew up and attended public schools in Miami, Florida. After high school, he worked at a variety of jobs ranging from factory helper to printer. Later, after serving three years in the U. S. Coast Guard and receiving an honorable discharge, Newman joined the staff of the *Miami News* where he worked as a reporter. In 1967, he moved to California where he served on the staffs of the *Redwood City Tribune*, *Burlingame Advance-Star* and *San Jose Mercury News*, taking time in between to earn a bachelor's degree. He subsequently received a Master of Science (psychology) degree from the University of Wisconsin-Milwaukee in 1973. He also served as an adjunct faculty member at West Valley College in Saratoga, California from 1973-1983.

In 1983, Newman founded The Newsletter Group which for two decades produced employee and customer newsletters for high tech firms in Silicon Valley. He also published *The Newman Report*, a hotel sales and marketing newsletter.

Among notable achievements, Newman has received the American Political Science Association Award for Distinguished Reporting of Public Affairs; San Francisco Press Club, best news story; South Bay Press Club, best feature story; the Associated Press News Executives Conference, best feature story; and the State Bar of California's Golden Medallion Media Award for outstanding reporting on the administration of justice.

He has been a volunteer in Big Brothers, a Little League coach and rental housing mediator for the City of Mountain View, California. He also served as a trip leader for the Sierra Club, volunteer tutor for Literacy Volunteers of Pima County and an elementary school mentor for the Interfaith Coalition for the Homeless.

He was the founder of Project One Hour One Child, a volunteer tutoring program for at-risk elementary school children.

Newman is the author of *101 Ways To Be A Long-Distance Super-Dad... or Mom, Too!* (Blossom Valley Press), a handbook for long-distance parents and *Things I Know Now That I Wish I'd Known Then — 150 Tips for Living Smarter* (Robert D. Reed Publishers).

Newman and his wife, Sondra, live in Tucson, Arizona.

Made in United States
Troutdale, OR
11/03/2026

56852537R00198